155.9
Vincennes Lincoln High School

4432
Coping when a parent has cancer
Strauss, Linda Leopold

W9-CKH-222

#21989

155.9 Strauss, Linda
STR   Leopold

Coping when a
   parent has cancer

$12.95

DATE		

PROPERTY OF

Lincoln High School Library

© THE BAKER & TAYLOR CO.

Being honest with your parents and other family members —even with yourself—about your feelings is not easy. But it will help you. And this book can help you get started. In it you will find straightforward discussions of a variety of issues that other teens in your situation have had to deal with: concerns about the future; about your role in the family versus your need for space and independence; about the need to grieve; about the effect of your parent's cancer on relationships with your friends; about your own physical and mental health; about drugs and alcohol; about visiting in hospitals; about the possibility of your parent's death and ways you and your family might cope with it. There is also a chapter on the special problems of children of single-parent families. You can use the book as an ice-breaker with your parents ("I read this book and it said . . ."). Or, as you read, you might want to mark the pages that you would like to discuss and either give the book to your parents or leave it around where they will be sure to see it. Maybe then they will bring up the subjects you want to talk about if you are uncomfortable about bringing them up yourself. The important thing is for you to be able to talk to someone about your parent's cancer and your own reactions to it. If you can't talk to one person, find another. But try to get your feelings out so that they don't swamp you. Cancer is not a problem anyone should have to handle alone.

Many things about cancer make it a particularly stressful disease to live with, but most people find the uncertainty the hardest to bear. A person seems well, then suddenly is sick again. A treatment works, then stops working. Unfortunately, medical science does not know enough about how various cancers act to be able to predict outcomes reliably. Doctors seldom make predictions, and never promises. But a medication that fails to work at first may also suddenly become effective. Tumors have been known to shrink spontaneously. A bed ridden patient may return full time to a demanding job. So the opposite side of that uncertainty is hope, if you look at it the right way. And hope is essential. Never forget in the days and weeks ahead that it is possible to live with cancer, and it is also possible to live with dying, if in the end you have to.

"We're doing better, Mom and I," says Kim, whose father died after a long battle with his cancer. "Mom has her bad days when she doesn't seem to cope with it real well, but even then you can talk to her now without it getting her real upset. And I feel better too, most of the time."

"I told a joke at the hospital the other day," says Michael, "and Dad started laughing, and then we both started cracking up and the nurse came running in we were laughing so hard. And the joke wasn't even that funny. But everyone was so quiet and serious when we first found out, Dad said it depressed him. It's better this way."

"I think we're going to make it," Kim says softly.

Kim is right. She and Michael are both survivors. You also will find the strength you need in the days ahead. You can make it, too.

CHAPTER 1

What Is Cancer and How Is It Treated?

It may seem that all your family's time and attention these days is consumed by your parent's illness and the frantic search for ways to beat it. Cancer is all anyone ever thinks about, but still you don't understand what is going on. There may be a number of reasons for your confusion. Perhaps your parents don't really understand the situation yet. Being presented with a diagnosis of cancer is such a big shock to a person that many patients defend themselves psychologically by simply not hearing what the doctor is telling them. Or they may get nervous and forget what was said. Or the explanation given to them may not have been clear, and they need to talk and ask further questions until they understand all the implications of their illness and the proposed plans for treating it. Perhaps your parents need to understand better what is going on in their lives before they can explain it to you.

When Carin's father came home and told her that her mother was going to need surgery for breast cancer, Carin ran out of the room. She spoke to her father later that night and asked him if her mother was going to be all right. "I don't know," her father said. "But we have to be optimistic." Carin was afraid to think too much about the surgery —it made her feel sick. Her father tried to explain that there were new ways of treating cancer, but all Carin could think about was, What would her mother look like after the operation? Would she still seem like her mother? Carin didn't hear much of anything her father said.

Perhaps you, too, were shocked at the word "cancer" being applied to your mother or father and too upset to sort out the information you were given at first about your parent's illness. That is not surprising: Some news takes adjusting to. But eventually you need some solid facts about your parent's illness because otherwise you have no way of understanding or preparing for the changes that inevitably will take place in your life. You may be worrying needlessly about some things. Or you may need to prepare yourself for some particularly difficult months ahead. Books like this one can be helpful in informing you, but cancer is really a variety of diseases with a variety of treatments. Each case is different. So although general information will apply *generally* to your parent's case, you will need further information to really know what is going on. Reading the pages that follow can help you to frame questions and understand answers. Just keep in mind that much is still not known about cancer and that every case has its own unique dynamics.

Some of you have parents who are easy to approach for information. Others have parents who think they are serving their children's best interests by shielding them from unpleasant details of illness and discussions about the uncertainties of the future. Still other parents may feel the need to protect their own privacy or may themselves not be prepared to face facts. You may then have to press for information, but don't be too afraid of upsetting your parents by asking for the facts. Ask one parent for the answers; if he or she can't or won't talk to you, ask the other. Explain to your parents that cancer affects the whole family; that you, too, are affected by the changes caused by illness; and that you need to know what to expect. If you can't get information from your parents, try talking to an aunt or uncle, to an adult friend of the family, to your guidance counselor at school, to your parent's doctor, to your own doctor. And if you find yourself hesitant about asking questions because you are afraid to hear the answers, that, too, is natural. But hard as it sometimes is to face facts, it usually helps to know.

Suppose you ask questions and get information, but you still don't understand what you have been told. That happens frequently, even to adults who are discussing cancer for the first time. *Oncology*, the medical specialty that deals with cancer, is a complex field, and doctors and nurses and medical technicians often use terms that sound totally foreign to patients and their families. If you or your parents get information that you don't understand, you should ask for an explanation. You might even want to take notes while someone is talking to you so that you can be sure you have got the facts right. Then you can ask questions later about the parts you don't understand. Don't forget that doctors and nurses are people just like you, and that cancer *can* be explained in terms that ordinary people can understand. The information below should be understandable (if it's not, ask someone for an explanation!) and help you get your education started.

What Is Cancer?

As was said above, many things are *not* known about cancer (including what causes it), but there are certain facts that will help you understand what is going on. Cancer is a group of more than one hundred diseases in which there is irregular growth of abnormal cells. In a healthy body cells are always dying and other cells are growing in an orderly fashion to replace them. This normal process goes on all the time. But sometimes something happens to change the physiology of cells in a particular part of the body, and those cells then start to multiply out of control. Eventually that place has more abnormal cells than healthy ones, and the abnormal ones start to crowd out and interfere with the functioning of the healthy ones. The abnormal growth of cells is cancer. Each kind of cancer has its own distinguishing characteristics, and a given kind of cancer may behave differently in different people. Cancerous cells are often called *malignant* (harmful) cells, as opposed to normal, harmless, or *benign* cells.

To repeat, cancer cells grow in an uncontrolled way. In a healthy body, normal cells are produced to replace older cells that die or wear out, but just enough new ones are produced to replace the old ones. Cancer cells don't automatically stop reproducing themselves, and that is what causes the problems. The cancer cells can reproduce either at the original site (usually in an ever-growing mass, or *tumor*) or by breaking away from that site and spreading to other parts of the body through the bloodstream or the lymphatic system. Then the cancer starts to grow in a new place in the body. (This process of spreading to distant parts of the body is called *metastasis*—the cancer is said to be *metastasizing.*[1]) But when a certain type of cancer spreads to another part of the body, it does not change its classification. For instance, if Carin's mother's breast cancer spread to her lungs, she would still have breast cancer metastasized to the lung, not lung cancer. This is not just a matter of playing with words, because the treatment for breast cancer is different from that for lung cancer. (There are also different kinds of breast cancers, lymphomas, etc.) Two people with cancer in the lungs might receive very different treatment, depending on where the cancer originated. That is why doctors try very hard to determine the original site of a cancer. It is also why you can't predict the kind of treatment your own parent will undergo based on the experience of your friend's mother or of the neighbor next door.

One more word about the spread of cancer: Even though it can spread rapidly through the body of the person who has it, *it cannot spread to other people.* You don't have to worry about hugging or kissing or being close in any way to a person who has cancer. You don't have to worry about your other parent's sleeping in the same bed as your ill parent. *Cancer is not a contagious disease.*

How Is Cancer Treated?

Once you understand a bit about what cancer is, it is easier to understand how it is treated. The four main methods of treatment—surgery, radiation, chemotherapy, and immunotherapy—all involve removing or killing or stopping the growth of the abnormal cells. Since even one remaining cell can multiply and cause the disease to recur, the ideal

---

[1] Sometimes you will hear people talk familiarly about these traveling cancer cells as "mets."

goal of treatment is to destroy every single cancer cell. Although methods now exist that could accomplish this, doctors have to limit and control their use or stretch out their application over time because of the harm the treatments cause to healthy tissue. In short, wonderful as it would be to be able to kill all the cancer cells right away with a super dose of some chemical, you can't do that because too strong a dose would kill the patient as well. A balance must be reached to find something effective enough to kill the cancer but not so strong that it also kills the healthy cells necessary to keep the patient alive.

Often the first treatment method used after a diagnosis of cancer is *surgery*—cutting out and removing the cancerous cells or tumor. *Radiation* is also used to shrink tumors, sometimes before surgery. Surgery and radiation are commonly used to treat cancers that are localized in a particular part of the body, and they may be all that is required to treat certain kinds of cancer. (Radiation works by changing the chemistry of the cancer cells, causing them either to die or to become incapable of dividing, or causing mutation of their genetic material so that they can reproduce, but not as functioning cancer cells. Radiation treatments are given in a carefully controlled way, so you don't have to worry afterward that your parent is radioactive or unsafe to be with.)

For cancers that are not localized, *chemotherapy* may be the first treatment recommended. Chemotherapy may also be used as a follow-up to radiation or surgery: The chemotherapy drugs or hormones circulate throughout the body in the bloodstream to take care of any unseen cancer cells left behind by the other treatments. Chemotherapy, radiation, and surgery may all be used at various other times in the treatment to stop or slow the growth of cancer cells or to alleviate symptoms. *Immunotherapy* works in a slightly different way, introducing substances into the body that bolster the body's own natural defenses in the hope that the body will itself be able more effectively to fight off the cancer.

Medical scientists are also constantly investigating new ways of treating cancer, and sometimes patients are offered the chance to try an experimental treatment. These experimental programs are controlled by the federal government, and no patient would be treated under such a program unless there were at least some hope that the treatment would benefit him. But the experimental treatments also hold some risks. Usually patients who are given the option of trying these methods are patients who have not responded to standard treatment methods, or who are very ill, or who have a kind of cancer that traditionally has a fairly low cure rate with standard treatments. Your parent's doctor would be the best person to recommend such a treatment. The National Cancer Institute has a toll-free number (1–800–4–CANCER)[2] to provide information to cancer patients and their families about both standard and experimental programs, which can then be checked out with the family's doctor. But remember: Although a new program or a newly publicized "cure" may seem ideal when you first hear about it, there are many stages in the development of these treatments and many differences in individual cancer cases. Traditional methods will most likely turn out to be the best choice for your parent.

As a cancer patient, your parent may also participate in a "study." The drugs used in studies are not experimental drugs. They are medicines that have already been deter-

---

[2] In Washington, D.C., and suburbs, call 636–5700; in Alaska, call 1–800–638–6070; in Hawaii, call 524–1234 on Oahu or that same number collect on other islands.

mined to be *at least as* effective as older medicines, but they are being studied further so that doctors can determine the results of their use in a larger population than is normally used to test experimental drugs. Studies are different from experimental treatments and should not be confused with them. Many patients with excellent chances for recovery participate in studies.

In combination with the treatments mentioned above, many patients nowadays use "mind over cancer" methods such as relaxation, hypnosis, self-hypnosis, biofeedback, and visual imagery. Although hard information is still lacking to support these methods as treatments on their own, a growing number of doctors believe that they can be useful in conjunction with more traditional methods. That is also true of various diet programs. However, patients and their families are warned to be cautious of "fad" cures, some of which can do more harm than good, especially when used *instead* of medically approved methods that have a scientifically based chance of controlling the cancer.

To review, the chief treatment methods for cancer are surgery, radiation, chemotherapy, and immunotherapy, either individually or in some combination. The particular combination of treatments, and the order of their use, is sometimes called the *protocol* of treatment. A protocol is like a recipe, and the ingredients are chosen to achieve the maximum kill of cancer cells. If one method of medication doesn't get all the cells, it is hoped that the next one will. The choice of treatment method or protocol has to do with such things as the kind of cancer (for example, certain types of tumors are very sensitive to radiation, others are not), the location of a tumor, the condition of the patient, how much the disease has spread, and the patient's tolerance to specific medications. Treatment may be changed during the course of the disease. Sandy remembers how excited his family was when the chemotherapy recommended by the doctor seemed to be controlling his father's disease. His father was back at work, and everything was almost like old times. And then out of the blue the report came one day that the doctor needed to change the medication, and Sandy immediately feared the worst. The doctor didn't seem too upset, though. He told Sandy's family that it wasn't at all uncommon to change from one treatment method to another, to change doses or change medicines, even to stop all treatment for a while, and that the changes didn't necessarily mean that there had been a setback. Sandy was greatly relieved, although he wished the doctor had told them about these possibilities ahead of time.

Side Effects of Treatment

Because the drugs and other substances used to kill cancer cells must be so strong, sometimes the patient has to put up with unpleasant side effects. The side effects represent damage to normal, healthy cells as a result of treatment. (Some of the newer experimental treatment forms try to "tag" the malignant cells in some way so that the chemicals used seek out only the cells they are intended to destroy, and not the healthy ones. This kind of targeting is designed to reduce side effects.) Side effects may include skin irritation, nausea, hair loss, fatigue, weight loss, mood changes, bloating, mouth sores, fever, confusion, and increased vulnerability to other diseases.

Sometimes side effects can seem worse than the cancer, and it is hard not to resent the fact that they are necessary. Laura's father, for example, was discovered to have cancer as part of a routine checkup. He had not been feeling sick at all before he went to the doctor. But as a result of the chemotherapy begun by the doctor, suddenly Laura's father was feeling extremely weak and nauseated and feverish. It almost seemed as if he got sick as a result of going to the doctor, even though of course that wasn't true.

It is not surprising that patients and their families sometimes get discouraged with long and wearing treatments. But often unpleasant side effects can be alleviated by sensitive scheduling of treatments, by relaxation exercises, hypnosis, and mental imagery, and by such methods as keeping the patient's scalp very cold during treatment to reduce hair loss. Some people suffer no serious side effects at all. Others feel sick and weak for a day or so after each treatment, then feel fine the rest of the time. Even if your parent gets very sick, however, it is important to keep in mind that however unpleasant these treatments are, their purpose is to give your parent a chance of being well. In fact, sometimes patients and their families take a certain comfort in the treatments because they represent something actual and positive that is being done to fight the cancer. They may also feel nervous or depressed after a course of treatments is finished because it seems as if the patient is being left on his own to do the fighting, but this anxiety usually goes away as further checkups confirm continued control of the disease.

Remission and Cure

Can the cancer cells actually be destroyed by these treatments? Sometimes they can. At first the doctors use the word *remission*, which means that the disease has been brought under control or rolled back, its progress halted. A remission can be partial or complete. If it is complete, all symptoms and signs of the disease are gone—the doctors, in all their tests, can't find any signs of cancerous cells. If remission is partial, some of the signs and symptoms are gone.

Even in complete remission some cancerous cells may remain in the body inactive and undetected, so doctors don't use the word *cure* until a patient's disease has been in remission long enough to make them fairly certain that the cancer has been destroyed completely. The time required for that varies with different kinds of cancer. A patient deemed "cured" is considered to have the same life expectancy as other persons of the same age and sex who have never had cancer. It does not mean that he or she will never get cancer again. It means, however, that he or she is *no more likely* to get it or die from it than anyone else in the particular statistical group.

A word here about recurrence: News that your parent is showing signs of disease after the cancer has been in remission for a time can be as hard to take as hearing the cancer diagnosis in the first place. Sometimes it can be even harder. But a recurrence is not a sign that all is lost. The most important thing is catching the likely recurrences in time. One reason that cancer patients have lots of checkups is that with proper supervision and treatment a person can live with certain kinds of cancer for years. In fact, many cancer patients live longer and better lives than they might with other diseases such as chronic heart problems, kidney failure, and certain lung diseases. It is important to keep remembering that cancer, although it sometimes does cause death, is not *necessarily* a death sentence. More and more it is being considered a chronic disease, a disease you can live with.

"The Big C"

"All disease is a misfortune," say Paul A. and Marilee Williams in an article in the *American Cancer Society Cancer Book*, and "cancer is one misfortune among many, but it does not warrant the singular horror and hopelessness with which it was once regarded. Times have changed greatly, as have attitudes, but even so, cancer evokes a fear that is not manifest in other diseases."[3]

Perhaps you were afraid even to read this chapter at first because of what you thought you might find out about cancer and your parent's chances. Many people are reluctant to say the word "cancer" out loud—they call it "the big 'C'"—as if just by voicing the word they might be inviting some great catastrophe upon themselves. Do you feel the same way? If you do, you might try saying the word "cancer" out loud right now ten or twenty times, until it becomes only a word to you. Say it loud and clear. Conquering that taboo is a good first step toward facing reality. After all, your parent *does* have cancer, and you and your family have to deal with it. The sooner the word gets into your working vocabulary, the sooner you will be able to start using it to get information and make plans and share worries—to deal honestly and constructively with whatever you have to deal with.

Cancer is not a plague or a curse; it is an illness, a disease that your mother or father has and that he or she will be battling with the help of modern medicine. Thinking of cancer in these terms will help you to remember that your parent is still your parent—the same person after the diag-

---

[3] Williams, Paul A. and Marilee, "The Treatment Team," *The American Cancer Society Cancer Book*, Arthur I. Holleb, M.D. ed. (Garden City, N.Y.: Doubleday & Company, Inc., 1986), p. 112.

nosis as before, with the same strengths and needs, quirks and talents, likes and dislikes. And your sick parent is also the one who knows his illness best. Try talking to him about how it feels, how he needs or wants to be treated, what the doctors have planned. Then you, in turn, might want to share some of the information you have just read— perhaps he or she has some questions he is wondering about, too.

With all the information you gather, however, the question that will be foremost in your mind is: Will my parent get well? And unfortunately no one can tell you that. "Death" is another word that you need to practice saying out loud—not because your parent necessarily will die of cancer, but because you need to face and talk about that possibility. More discussion of death is given in later chapters. But first the focus is on living, because that is where most patients and their families want and need to keep their attention. What is it like living with cancer? Are you able to handle it? How should you behave?

Life is full of unknowns right now, but be assured that the stresses and uncertainties of cancer *can* be handled. And try to leave room for hope. Your family's history, after all, is still being written.

CHAPTER 2

What About Me?

That may be the question that popped into your mind when you learned that your mother or father had cancer. It may still be at the top of your mind where you are aware of it, or it may be buried down deep because you feel guilty thinking about yourself and your own worries at a time when someone you love is so sick and needs your attention. But you needn't feel guilty. It is normal and natural at your age to worry about what is going to happen to you, especially when you are faced with cancer, an illness that is particularly frightening to most people. The fear of being abandoned is a very basic human feeling and one that you are not too old to be experiencing. Even if your sick parent is responding well to therapy and your other parent is young and strong and healthy, you may still be wondering who would take care of you if something happened to both your parents. After all, if cancer struck one parent without warning, why couldn't something equally unexpected happen to the other? Of course, chances are that it won't. But the fear is still an understandable one and needs to be addressed. You need to know what to expect.

Who Will Take Care of You?

That decision may already have been made by your parents, perhaps when you were very small. Many parents make wills as a matter of routine, not just to divide up property but because they want to choose who will take care of their children if anything happens to them. Other parents make less formal agreements with family members or close friends who agree to raise their children if both parents die while the children still need care. In any case you will not, as a child, have to support yourself or care for your younger brothers or sisters on your own. Under the law you are considered to require the care and support of adults until you reach the age of adulthood.

If your parents have never discussed these matters with you, you may need to raise the subject yourself. Lynette, encouraged by her support group leader to bring up the matter of her care with her family, reported back with great delight that *all* of her adult brothers and sisters had said they would want her, and "I'll go with whichever one gets to me first, I guess!" Sarah's mother showed her a loving letter from an aunt saying that Sarah and her brothers and sister would always have a home with her if something happened. Richard's parents had made no plans but recognized the need to do so. Although their first thought was that Richard should go to an out-of-state uncle, Richard said he really would want to stay and finish up at his present high school if he could. So his parents said they would try to make arrangements with his grandfather, who lived nearby. One good reason to bring up the subject for discussion now is so that you can be involved in some of the decisions. You have particular concerns and preferences. Be as honest and open as you can about them with your parents.

The subject of your future care is difficult to raise—especially when someone is ill—and not all parents will respond positively to your bringing it up. They may think that discussing such plans means that you are giving up or being morbid or even jinxing your ill parent. But you need not feel guilty about wanting to be reassured about your future and wanting to be involved in decisions that will affect you. It will help to be able to attach some names and places to your images of the future, no matter how remote the various possibilities may be. And thinking about someone's death cannot cause it to happen. You are simply being realistic in facing the possibility and trying to get a handle on what it would mean for you.

Security is a very important issue for a person in your situation. As a child you have been accustomed to looking to your parents for the security that every child needs. Now, not only has illness undermined that sense of endless strength that most children assign to their parents, but it is likely that your parents have become so involved in an endless round of doctors' appointments and treatments or hospitalizations that they are not even around to offer you comfort and support when you most need it. "It was like suddenly losing not just Mom but both my parents to the cancer," remembers Sam. He also remembers feeling scared and lonely—and angry at his father for not recognizing his need. "Even when my father got home," he says, "he spent most of the time comforting my little sister because he thought she was too young to really understand what was going on. But I was just as scared as Allie was. Nobody in our family had ever been sick before, not to mention in a hospital. And I'd get so mad at Allie because she wouldn't behave for me and I'd get mad at Dad because he kept saying, 'I'll let you know as soon as I know something,' except nobody ever seemed to know anything—at least they didn't tell *me*. But everyone still expected me to take care of everything, like I didn't have feelings, too."

Sam's reaction is a very normal one, although many teens in his situation won't admit to themselves how angry they feel because they think they are supposed to suppress their needs in response to the greater crisis in the family. They don't understand that a diagnosis of cancer affects the whole family, and each person's needs are important in terms of how the family deals with the illness. Not everyone's needs can be met fully at any given time—sometimes the parent who is the caregiver has no choice but to stay at the hospital with the patient, and sometimes the children have to wait for attention because the demands of the illness must be met right away—but no one needs to feel guilty about his feelings or about being angry and upset that his needs are not being met.

It is important to remember also that sometimes others simply don't *know* how you are feeling, that they don't know what you need until you tell them. You can get angry at them for that, but ask yourself if that air of confidence and competence you have been working so hard at might not have fooled everyone into thinking you have it all under control. Sam's father might truly have felt that Sam was coping well, or he might have thought that Sam would get defensive if he tried to comfort him. Or he might have been so distraught and preoccupied with his own needs that he didn't notice that Sam needed help.

In any case, Sam needed to tell him. Sam, like many other fifteen-year-olds, was not accustomed to opening up to his father or to verbalizing his needs and his feelings. At a time in his life when he was just getting used to being on his own more and *not* going to his parents for everything, it was not easy for him to switch gears and admit that he needed emotional support. But his mother's illness was a new situation in his family that required new coping mechanisms, new ways of doing things. Some children of cancer patients signal that they need help by misbehaving and getting into trouble, but asking for help directly is a much more mature and constructive way of dealing with what is bothering you. Says Rosalie, another support group member, "It's a good idea to talk to one or both of your parents—whoever's easiest to talk to—and find out exactly what's happening and let them know exactly how you feel. No matter how hard you think it's going to be or how much you hate to talk to your parents, I think it's something you have to do and in the long run it'll benefit you a lot."

Expressing Your Feelings

Some children are reluctant to express their needs because they believe that showing their feelings will somehow undermine the strength of the family. In our society being strong is often equated incorrectly with not breaking down, not showing emotion. "I felt like I had to be strong for Carol and my other sister and for Mom," said sixteen-year-old Marcy. "I thought that crying was weakness, and I had to show them that it was going to be okay, that no matter what happened we would get along." Marcy knew that if she started crying in front of her mother and sisters they would probably break down, too. And she was undoubtedly right. What she didn't realize was that crying would almost certainly have been a welcome release for all the members of her family. In many families where one member has cancer, each person in the family is afraid to show his fear and emotion to the others, and each person bears his burden alone. The tragic part of this behavior is that it makes everyone lonely as well as sad, and it makes the burden of the illness harder, not easier, to bear. Marcy found that she couldn't release her emotions even when she was by herself. "Even when I was alone," she said, "I felt like I couldn't cry, I couldn't let that tough side of myself get weak." The point is that Marcy *needed* to vent her feelings, and doing so would not have hurt her family in the least. Luckily, Marcy learned that eventually. "I wanted to be strong," she admits, "but I know now that if it gets to the point where you're hurting yourself because you're not able to express your emotions, that's bad. You have to cry. I mean, it's sad."

Families whose members do express emotions freely have a lot of extra pluses going for them when it comes to coping with a family crisis like cancer. You might have to take the lead in your family and reach out to someone by acknowledging and expressing your needs. It's worth a try. It will take some emotional pressure off of you, and it's a good way to start the family process of sharing feelings.

As we have seen, many children of cancer patients feel lonely and frightened as a result of lack of attention from their parents. Others, however, find that their parents worry about them all the time and keep them *too* close to home. It is natural when one family member is very sick to worry that something might also happen to other people in the family. Just as children often start worrying about their healthy parent, parents may start fussing unnecessarily over their children. You may suddenly be required to come home earlier, or to check in more often. Some of the requirements may have to do with a real need for you to be on call, to be available to help out. But if you are convinced that your parents really are worrying about you unnecessarily and are restricting your independence unfairly out of *their* need, not out of legitimate concern for your safety, you may need to have a talk with them. They may not even realize they are behaving that way.

What About You?

Emotions, as you can see, become complicated when there is cancer in the family. You will probably find many things in your life to feel angry about. Your parents are never available to give you and your friends rides or to come to school activities as they used to, or to help you with homework. They make promises that illness forces them to break. An older brother or sister is suddenly put in a position of authority in the household and thinks he or she can boss you around. ("I didn't know who was in charge," complained Evan. "One of my brothers might tell me to do something. Then my mother would come home and tell me I shouldn't have done it. Who was I supposed to listen to?") Your father suddenly decides that everything in the house has to be kept perfectly neat in your mother's absence and yells and screams if he comes home and finds one towel out of place, even though you've spent all afternoon making dinner and doing everyone's laundry. Your little brother whines constantly and gets on your nerves. You can't have friends over because your father gets exhausted when there's too much noise. You need a dress for the prom and have to shop for it alone. You worry about who will be able to look at colleges with you. Will you even be able to go to college? Will you ever be able to have any normal kind of life at all?

It is no wonder you feel angry. You have a right to feel angry. Your life is being disrupted, and your parent's life is threatened, and all the rules that once applied seem to be turned inside out. Many children of cancer patients are appalled to find themselves feeling angry at the parent who is sick, but that kind of anger is a perfectly normal reaction, too. You don't have to feel guilty about those feelings or to think there is something wrong with you for having them.

Most teenage children of cancer patients experience them to one degree or another. It is also normal for you still to be concerned about clothes and sports and friends and whether or not you will make the staff of the school paper. Your life is not supposed to stop because your parent has cancer, although it may sometimes seem as if it has. And certainly your life will change in many significant ways. But underneath it all you are still the same fourteen-year-old or sixteen-year-old or nineteen-year-old. Give yourself permission to look after your own needs once in a while. You are allowed to have fun when you can. Give yourself a break.

Money Problems

Although each of you will have specific problems of concern to you, certain categories of problems are encountered by many teenage children of cancer patients. One major issue is finances. You and your parents may start worrying about money right away, especially if the parent who has cancer is the breadwinner or contributes significantly to the family income. You may worry about whether the other parent alone will be able to support you. Some parents have insurance that covers emergencies such as temporary loss of income or large medical bills or the death of the breadwinner of the family. But the medical expenses of cancer treatment (even with insurance) can be overwhelming, and most families have to make financial adjustments of one kind or another. Medical bills combined with the loss of income can turn a family's budget upside down, and financial worries combined with the stress of illness can put tremendous strain on a family. Sometimes the entire lifestyle of a family must change. You may be asked to go to work to pay your own expenses or, if you are old enough, to contribute to the family income. Or you might have to take care of your younger brothers and sisters after school or help with household chores because your mother has to get a job outside the home. Your camp plans or travel plans may have to be canceled. Your family might even have to move.

Whatever the change in the family financial situation, it can be hard on you. It may be a matter of having less spending money than your friends and feeling angry or embarrassed because you can't do all the things they do, or you may be facing the postponement of college plans. But many teenage children of cancer patients compound their problems because they do not know what the situation really is. This can work two ways. If they are unaware that money is in short supply, they may unwittingly trigger a parent's anger by asking for money that was always willingly given before. Or they may unnecessarily deprive themselves by assuming that things are worse than they are. Saul was a table tennis champion, but he almost didn't sign up for a prestigious tournament because he didn't have enough money of his own for travel expenses and didn't feel he should put an extra burden on his mother by asking her to help him. As it turned out, however, Saul's parents wanted him to go. To them, the expense of his participating seemed well worthwhile, and in fact Saul's father used the tournament as his goal for getting out of the hospital. The whole family wound up celebrating Saul's father's remission by going to the tournament and watching Saul play. But Saul only found out by asking his parents.

You, too, won't know what your own family situation is until you ask. Be honest and reasonable with your parents about your needs, and ask them to be honest and reasonable with you. They may not be able to give you everything you feel you need, but by discussing the situation you can let them know your problems and perhaps figure out some priorities. Even if the problems can't be solved, just talking about them can lighten the burden. Some parents are reluctant to talk about financial matters with children, however, and others may get defensive about not having enough money to go around. You may have to explain why you are asking. You can use this book to help you.

One of your worries about the family's financial situation might also be that there won't be enough money to pay for your sick parent's medical care. But be reassured that sick people are almost never turned away from hospitals for lack of funds. If your family does have serious financial concerns, a hospital social worker or one of the local cancer agencies listed in your telephone book may be able to help you find solutions to your problems. You can also call 1–800–4–CANCER for suggestions. (See p. 12 for phone numbers in Washington D.C., Alaska, and Hawaii.)

Taking on the Parental Role

Another large issue for teenage children of cancer patients is the role they must often take on as a "substitute parent." When both parents are out of the house a lot during treatments or hospitalizations, or when the sick parent is very ill at home and the other parent is out working, the oldest child often gets the job of keeping the household running. This becomes a great responsibility for the young person to bear, and it frequently interferes with his or her own schoolwork or job or social life. The parents, moreover, may not even seem to realize how much he or she is doing—often they seem to expect even more. "I couldn't do anything that my friends could," said Walt. "They all had their licenses and were driving around all afternoon, and I had to come home right after school every day to take

care of my two little brothers because my mother had to go
to work. And I had to get dinner and do the yardwork and
everything. There was no way I could stay on the soccer
team because I couldn't make the practices. I knew that,
but it would've been nice if I could have gone to a game
once in a while. But I had to take my brothers to *their* practices and then stay with them until my mother got home
from visiting Dad at the hospital. Which sometimes wasn't
until nine or ten at night."

John says that the worst part for him was having to give
up his after-school job. "I really liked that job," he said.
"And I liked earning my own money and not having to ask
anyone if I wanted to buy something. I hated asking Mom
for money—it made me feel about two years old. And it
was the same with going out. I had to ask ahead every time
I wanted to go somewhere because Mom didn't always feel
well enough to take care of my little brother. I felt like I
was going backwards—you know, like I was never going to
get out of the house and live my own life."

Ruthie didn't like the responsibilities put on her at first,
but then she got used to her new role and took pride in
being able to keep things going the way her mother would.
The hard part for her was when her mother came home
from the hospital and expected to take over again. "She'd
get mad at me when I'd tell one of my sisters to pick up
after herself, and she'd make me go to bed like before and
have to ask permission for everything. I'd been acting like
an adult, and now they treated me like a baby again."

Maria, who was a senior, got through the second year of
her mother's illness knowing that she was about to gradu-
ate and go to college; but Teresa, the next oldest in the
family, didn't want her to go. Maria felt caught in the
middle: "There's so much that Teresa and I do around
the house, and my younger sister isn't old enough to do any

PROPERTY OF
SOUTH KNOX SCHOOL CORP.

of that stuff, so Teresa's going to have a lot to pick up, and I don't know how she's going to do it sometimes. And it's kind of a conflict, because sometimes I want to leave and she says I shouldn't want to."

Handling the Pressure

The pressure can come from anywhere—from brothers or sisters, from parents, from aunts and uncles, from neighbors, from family friends, from within yourself. Sometimes it's directly stated ("You're going to have to start doing more around the house"); sometimes less direct ("When your grandmother was sick and in bed, I took care of her for five whole years and *I* never complained."). Even compliments you receive for doing a good job can seem to put enormous pressure on you. Some children get so angry and overwhelmed that they actually wind up running away from home. Others become depressed or develop physical symptoms of various kinds—headaches, hives, stomachaches. The best way to protect yourself is by not allowing the tension and anger to build up unexpressed.

Note here that expressing anger does not necessarily mean yelling at someone. Anger can be expressed in reasonable tones; it can be vented by telling your parents that you have a problem; it can be relieved by getting some hard physical exercise, or pounding on a pillow, or complaining to a sympathetic friend. You may also be able to work out some constructive solutions to the burdens placed on you by your parent's illness. Maybe a neighbor or a relative can take over for you one day a week. Or a friend can baby-sit for your younger brothers and sisters while you go out. Simple things like getting fast food once or twice a week, or using paper plates occasionally, can do a lot to lighten the burden of preparing a daily meal. If sickroom duties are what you hate most, maybe your younger sister or brother is better at it and you can do more housework or yardwork instead. Maybe you are even keeping the house *too* clean, and you can let some things go occasionally.

Remember that trying to work out ways to make your burden of responsibility more tolerable does not mean that you are not being a good son or daughter. Don't let anyone put a load of guilt on you for speaking up. The idea is not to get out of helping but to keep from burning out. If you put too much strain on yourself you are likely to wind up more a problem to your family than a help. Not all parents understand that, however. You may have to ask a relative or a family friend or a school counselor to intervene for you, to speak up for the legitimacy of your needs.

It is hard to be a teenager. It is a time of life characterized by conflicting loyalties, conflicting feelings, conflicting needs. You love your family, yet you are working to separate from them, to become a capable, functioning adult. And hard as it is to be a teenager under normal circumstances, it is even harder to be the teenage child of a cancer patient, because the demands of the cancer—both in time and emotional commitment—tend to keep you closer to home than you ordinarily would need to be at that stage of your life. It may seem like a no-win situation. If you pull away from your family, you feel guilty. If you remain too closely involved with them, you feel anger and resentment. It seems disloyal to think about your own future, but you can't help dreaming of escape.

But it is *not* disloyal to think about your future. You may have to defer your plans a bit, but it will help to have them as a goal. It is natural to want to get on with your life—it was natural for Maria, in the example given earlier, to want to leave home and go to college, and it was also natural for her sister (and her parents) not to want her to go. When Maria does go away, she will probably feel a bit guilty about not being at home any longer, but that will be normal, too. Emotions and family relationships are always complicated, and cancer complicates them further. A person can feel many things—even opposite things—at the same time. You can love your parents and want to help them and also feel that staying at home all the time and putting your life on hold is driving you crazy. You will do better in the long run if you accept the negative feelings as well as the positive ones. Try to remember that strength means being honest about feelings. It does not mean burying your concerns and keeping them to yourself.

Bill of Rights for Family Members

Everyone knows and accepts that cancer patients have problems. It is not as well recognized, however, that their families may need help, too. Cancer Family Care of Cincinnati, in recognition of that need, has drawn up a "Bill of Rights" for family members of cancer patients that includes the following items. It will help you to read them and to refer back to them from time to time.

I have the right to enjoy my own good health without feeling guilty. It is not my fault that someone I love has cancer...

Even if I am a child I have a right to know what is going on in our family. I have a right to be told the truth about the cancer in words I can understand.

I do not always have to agree with someone just because he or she has cancer. I can get angry at the patient without always feeling guilty, because sickness does not stop someone from being a real person.

I have the right to feel what I feel..., not what someone else says I "should" feel.

I have the right to look after my own needs, even if they do not seem as great as the patient's. I am permitted to take "time out" from the cancer without feeling disloyal.

I have the right to get outside help for the patient if I cannot manage all the responsibilities of home care myself.

I also have the right to get help for *myself*, even if others in my family choose not to get help.[1]

As you can see, this Bill of Rights was written for all family members, not just for teenagers. You may want to show it to others in your family. They are very likely to be sharing many of your feelings—even the negative ones— and they too need to know that they have a right to feel that way.

What about you? Having a parent with cancer doesn't cancel out your own needs. You are not showing lack of concern for your sick parent, or loving him or her any less, if you consider your own needs. Certainly your parent's illness must take precedence sometimes, and at times you have to endure bitter disappointment, bear more responsibility than you should at your age, change or sacrifice your own plans to cope with a family crisis. But you will be better armed to deal with these things if you acknowledge your own needs, ask for some comfort, vent some frustration. You have a right for your own life to continue. You are important, too.

---

[1] "Bill of Rights" for Cancer Patients and their Families, Cancer Family Care, Inc., Cincinnati, Ohio. Reprinted with permission.

CHAPTER 3

Learning About Grieving

All people suffer losses from time to time in their lives, and it is natural to deal with loss by grieving. It is likely that you have been feeling loss from the time you learned that your mother or father had cancer. You have suffered loss of security, maybe loss of the presence of one or both of your parents from the house much of the time, loss of an accustomed way of life. Your sick parent is experiencing losses, too—some the same as yours, others different, because he or she is the patient. Cancer patients feel grief over the loss of an organ or a body part as a result of surgery; feel a loss of attractiveness as the result of various side effects of treatment; feel the loss of valued relationships, because some people can't deal with a person who has cancer; feel the loss of their role as breadwinner, or loss of independence. Grieving is a natural, healthful process that helps people deal with their losses and move beyond them. In fact, people who suffer a serious loss need to grieve in order to get well.

Stages of Grieving

People who have studied the process of grieving have found that different feelings are involved in different stages of grieving. The first stage is usually *shock and denial.* Perhaps you remember feeling that way when you were told that your mother or father had cancer. A frequent reaction is, "No, no, it can't be that serious," or, "This terrible thing can't be happening to me." This is a normal reaction, a way of protecting yourself against the shock of the news you have just received. It takes time to face the facts of an illness that can mean such a loss to you. Your parent may not look or act sick. It seems impossible to believe that someone could be perfectly well one minute and be told the next that he has such a serious disease. Maybe the doctors are wrong, you say to yourself. Maybe the hospital got someone else's test results. Maybe you have been asleep and will wake up and find this is all a dream.

But it is not a dream. And the next stage of grief, as reality sinks in, is often *anger.* The first question may be, "Why me?" The anger is not always directed logically— the grieving person may lash out at doctors, at family, at God, at life, at enemies, at friends. He may feel angry with himself for not having done something to prevent the situation. He may be grouchy and irritable and resent all the people in the world who are not sick and not suffering. He may be nasty to those who most want to help and comfort him.

A child whose parent dies of cancer often feels angry at the parent for getting sick and leaving him, even though he knows the parent can't help it. Sometimes children of very sick parents act out their anger by failing in school, stealing, fighting, refusing to visit at the hospital. Audra, whose mother had breast cancer, was furious at her mother because she knew that breast cancer sometimes runs in families. She blamed her mother for putting her, Audra, at risk. The anger she felt, although not rational, was still a natural and normal reaction. When life hurts you, you get angry. When you feel helpless and scared, you get angry. And when you have anger inside of you, you don't always let it out at the real object of your anger. Have you ever been really angry at a teacher at school and then gone home and yelled at your mother? Has one of your parents ever had a bad day at work and taken it out on you?

The next stage of grief that sometimes occurs is *bargaining*. Having accepted reality somewhat, the grieving person tries on some level to control it. He says to himself, "I promise never to get upset with my family again if only the cancer will go away." Or maybe he makes a bargain with God: "If I'm really good, if I get straight As at school, will You promise not to let things get any worse?" Sometimes children of cancer patients who wear themselves out running a perfect household for their parents may unconsciously be trying to fulfill their part of this kind of bargain. Of course, the truth is that your actions or thoughts or the words you say can't really control the progress of your parent's illness. But many people nevertheless feel as if they might.

As reality sets in, the next stage may be *depression*, in which the grieving person acknowledges his fate and all the losses involved. Numbness and rage are replaced by a sense of great sadness. The grieving person may be silent, withdrawn, impossible to cheer up. At this point in his grieving he wants and needs to feel his sorrow. It doesn't help when someone tries to cheer him up, because he has a legitimate reason for his sadness and needs to face it. This can be a difficult time for those who love him, who find it painful to see him so sad. All others can usefully do may be to stay with him without telling him that he should cheer up, and to listen when he expresses his feelings. It is a time when the grieving person is coming to terms with his loss, preparing to let go.

Feeling this pain and sadness, difficult as it is for everyone involved, seems to be necessary for the final stage of *acceptance*, a kind of sad peace when the grieving person realizes that little or nothing more can be done about the situation. He simply has to do the best he can with it. A sick patient working through grief about his own death may be very tired and weak at this point and ready to let go—the acceptance stage has been described as "the final rest before the long journey."[1] In the case of a person mourning the loss of a loved one, this stage may be the final preparation for letting go of the loved one, for moving ahead into a future without him or her.

If your parent's illness does become seriously life-threatening, you may see him or her moving through the stages listed above. People mourn the loss of their own life as well as the loss of those they love—and in much the same way. People coming to terms with the death of someone they love also go through those stages, sometimes while the loved person is ill, and sometimes after he or she dies. Not everyone goes though the stages in order—stages may be skipped or repeated or even overlapped—and not everyone goes through all the feelings in all the stages. People may go through some of the stages when the cancer is first diagnosed and then again if the cancer recurs after a remission. Sometimes, in the case of a long illness, the family may have reached the acceptance stage by the time

---

[1] Kubler-Ross, Elisabeth, *On Death and Dying* (New York: Macmillan, 1969), p. 113. Paperback edition.

the death occurs and will not need to do much additional mourning after the funeral. There are no hard and fast rules to the process, but it is generally considered that people must grieve, must go through this mourning, to deal constructively with their loss. When a very sick patient has done so, he can then die peacefully. And when his loved ones do so also, they can accept his death and heal and be happy again.

One additional word about acceptance: Not all very ill patients are able to reach that last stage of quiet peacefulness. Some may remain in the anger stage to the end, or in the depression stage, and their behavior may be difficult for their families to deal with. (It is also sometimes difficult for families to deal with the acceptance stage, because the patient may stop fighting and let go before the family is ready to let him go.) Don't be hard on your sick parent if he is not handling his illness the way you would want him to. It is in the end his illness, his fight. Just as no one should expect you to be a hero, you shouldn't expect your parent to be a hero. Your parent has a right to be human, too.

Differences in Grieving

It is important to remember, too, that despite what all people have in common in their grieving, everyone is also different. Everyone—including you—has a right to grieve according to his own schedule and in his own way. Don't let others put a burden of guilt on you because you are not grieving their way. In Marty's family there are six children, ranging in age from twelve years to nineteen. Marty and one sister were able to talk and cry together about their father's cancer. Marty's oldest brother, Tom, didn't talk much to the others, but he began spending a lot of time running and working out on the Nautilus machines at the

YMCA. Sean, the twelve-year-old, isolated himself in his room with his rock tapes almost every afternoon. Cathy, the fourteen-year-old, became very negative, refusing to do anything at all without an argument. Lisa, a year older than Cathy, made honors every quarter and won the sophomore prize for academic excellence at her high school. All of the children were deeply affected by their father's illness, but each dealt with it according to his or her age and personality and place in the family. Marty's mother had her own way of dealing with it also. A writer, she kept a journal of the family's experience, which she hoped to use some day as the basis for a book.

Some people do a lot of crying when they are sad. Others work off their grief and cry at night alone. Some people mourn directly; others find themselves breaking down more than usual in sad movies or over sad novels. Some people find laughing in the face of serious illness disrespectful; others find laughter the best medicine for both patient and loved ones. Your family has its own style, and it may be a style that others can't even comprehend.

When Eric's father went into the hospital for chemotherapy, some of the nurses were shocked when the family put a big sign on the door to his room, "Little Shop of Horrors." Eric's dad made them add an additional sign every morning that announced the "Horror of the Day." Sometimes the sign read "Nausea," sometimes "Exhaustion," once "Major Hair Loss." Although this kind of humor may not appeal to everyone, it helped Eric's family get through a very difficult time. Warren's family, on the other hand, was very religious and took comfort in praying together. Susannah's family hugged a lot and cried on the shoulders of the other families at the hospital.

The important thing is what works for you and your family. And don't forget that, as in Marty's family, different family members may have different styles of grieving. It might help you, when dealing with much younger brothers or sisters, to know that small children can't really comprehend death or the permanence of dying, no matter how much you try to explain it to them. Older children may feel numb or mourn intermittently because they are afraid of letting go altogether or being overwhelmed by grief. Others may try to appear cheerful all the time, as if a cheerful face could prevent something bad from happening. Still others, because of conflict with their parents, may be unwilling to express any feelings of sadness at all. It will help to try to be sensitive to other family members' styles and schedules of grief as well as your own. You can help each other: You are all in this grief together.

Sharing Grief

Understanding these things about grief may serve a number of purposes. For one thing, it may help you to understand better why your brothers and sisters act the way they do—you may see, for example, that their apparent lack of concern or their difficult behavior may not be lack of caring at all. Your parents, too, will be grieving, and it may help at times to know that their anger or bitterness or depression, although they may land on you, are not necessarily caused by you. But most important of all you will realize that you and your sick parent are having a lot of feelings in common.

Often a person who is very sick or dying wants to talk about what he is feeling, but everyone thinks it is necessary to present an optimistic face all the time and refuse to admit he or she is so sick. The patient may have moved on to the stage of confronting and accepting the illness, but the family, at least in the patient's presence, keeps on denying. Think how lonely it must be to know that you are very sick and want to share your feelings with someone and have no one who will let you talk about your illness.

You may, in fact, have experienced a similar situation if you ever tried to share your fears about your parent's illness with a friend and had the friend respond, "Oh, don't worry, I'm sure your mom (or dad) will be all right." That kind of answer may have sounded all right when you were still in the stage of denying, but how does it feel now that you are accepting the fact that your parent's condition may be very serious? Wouldn't it help more if someone would let you talk about your worries?

Your ill parent may be in that same predicament, wanting to talk and to grieve together with someone in the family, but afraid of upsetting the family by acknowledging that he or she knows the seriousness of the illness. If you can approach your parent honestly about what you are feeling, you may encourage him or her to share his feelings. You can begin to help him out of his loneliness, and you will be helping yourself as well.

Many people who fail for one reason or another to reach out to their loved ones when they are sick later regret that missed opportunity. Ellen's mother was in the hospital for cancer and then unexpectedly had a stroke. "She had her stroke, and then she was in the hospital all the time until she died," says Ellen sadly. "We never really got to talk with her or anything like that. . . I don't know if Dad knew that was a possibility. I wish I had talked to Mom more—about death and dying and her disease. I wish I had talked to her more. And then she had her stroke, and there was nothing I could do about it."

When family members do share their feelings, on the other hand, treasured moments can come from that sharing. Danny's father was close to death and the whole family was gathered around his bed, which happened to be in the living room of their home. Danny's two sisters had been crying all afternoon, but Danny was dry-eyed. Suddenly Danny said: "You know, there's something I've been wanting to say for a long time. I don't cry when I get upset, but I want Dad to know I love him as much as Sharon and Corrie do." That simple statement must have meant a great deal to Danny's father. And Danny himself was greatly comforted after his father's death by the knowledge that he had been able to express his feelings to his father, to tell him how much he cared.

Some people aren't good at putting things into words, however. Matt just couldn't express himself like that. But he was still able to show his sick father how much he loved him by giving him back rubs to make him more comfortable. Matt was the only one who could do the back rubs the way his father liked them. He came home right after school every afternoon to do them. And his father knew he cared.

You will have your own way of showing your caring to your parent. Try not to be frightened off by the seriousness of the illness, by the possibility or even the imminence of death. You don't have to be any different from what you are; remember again that you don't have to be a hero. Your genuine emotions will be a gift to your parent, a reaching out, a sharing. Just be yourself. Your parent is very likely concerned about you and how you are taking this illness, and it will help if you talk about it. Talking about death and your feelings about death with your sick parent may sound like a scary process, but getting started is the hardest part. And if you can cry and get angry together, you may all also be able to laugh and find peace together.

Occasionally doctors and family members may decide together not to tell a patient that he has cancer. This decision used to be more common, on the theory that people would give up hope if they knew they had a life-threatening disease. It is always a personal decision, based on the particular history and needs of a given patient. But today most professionals who work with cancer patients feel that each person should have the right to handle his own death, or the possibility of it, in his own way. Each person, they believe, should be allowed the opportunity to consider the end of his own life, to make his peace with his fate and his loved ones, and ultimately to say good-bye, if necessary, in his own way.

Allowing a person to consider the possibility of his death, however, should never be equated with taking hope away from that person. On the contrary, Elisabeth Kubler-Ross, one of the foremost experts in the field of death and dying, says that hope should be and is preserved in all the stages of dying, right up to the end. Even when the patient has reached the final stage of acceptance, she says, even after he no longer realistically expects a cure, he may still hope for a cure, a last-minute miracle, a scientific breakthrough. This hope can be very important to him, and it is important to his family, too.[2] No one has the right to take another person's hope away.

The Pain of Grief

Thinking and writing and talking about grief is one thing—feeling it is another, especially when you are in the middle of it and it seems as if it will never end. "Grief," one writer says, "can be described as an overwhelming and acute sense of loss and despair. The entire personality is helplessly engulfed in strong, sometimes frightening feel-

---

[2] Kubler-Ross, *On Death and Dying*, pp. 139–56.

ings. The individual can feel out of control as monstrous waves of emotions sweep over him or her. Tossed about on this emotional sea, the familiar and secure landmarks of life are no longer in their usual places, the old meanings do not apply, and the individual may see him or herself as the victim of forces outside of his or her control."[3]

One of the teen support group members describes her feelings in more specific, more physical terms. Her father, who was in the hospital, had for the first time admitted to himself that he might not get better and was making preparations to hand over the financial reins of the family to her mother. In the process he broke down and began to weep.

"I had never seen my daddy cry-cry," remembers Kari, "I mean *never*, not really, not as hard as he was then, and that hurt me. I just started getting nervous and I started getting sick—I almost got an ulcer, I got so worried. I mean, I could feel it in the pit of my stomach and it hurt so bad . . . , it was really painful. I hope I never have to go through that kind of pain again—it hurts too much—too, too much."

Sometimes that kind of pain seems as if it will go on forever, but it is necessary to feel it, to pass through it, in order to feel better again. In some cases the pain comes close on the heels of a loss; in others, it is delayed until an anniversary, or the sight of a particular photograph of the person you are mourning, or the sound of a piece of music triggers feelings and allows you to release your grief. For some people the pain of a loss seems almost constant, while for others it comes and goes. As you deal with your loss you will receive confusing messages from friends and relatives

---

[3] Stephenson, John A., *Death, Grief and Mourning: Individual and Social Realities* (New York: The Free Press, 1985).

who equate "doing well" or "being strong" with not expressing any unhappiness; but the truth is that it is only by expressing your grief and working through the pain that you will eventually be able to cast off your feelings of sadness and really start to heal. Not doing so can cause continuing unhappiness and even interfere with relationships later in life.

Unfortunately, the grief process cannot be hurried. The passage of time seems to be an essential part of healing. Be assured, though, that the pain of loss does ease eventually. Some people have an easier time with their bereavement; for others, it is harder. One student of bereavement makes a comparison between grief work and the way different people react to a wound or an infection: For some, the wound or infection is minor, with a smooth, predictable healing process, but others develop complications.[4] Some people may need professional help to unlock their feelings, whereas others benefit from the caring ear of a sympathetic friend. Since grief can feel very lonely, it helps to know that others understand and can give you the strength you need to get through it. Look for someone to help you. (See Chapter 4 for suggestions on how to find such a person.) Dealing with serious loss is not something you should ever be expected to do alone.

---

[4] Peretz, David, M.D., "Understanding Your Mourning: A Psychiatrist's View," in *But Not to Lose*, ed. Austin H. Kutscher (New York: Frederick Fell, Inc., 1969), pp. 137–138.

Finding Someone to Talk To

Having a parent sick with cancer is very hard to bear, but it is infinitely harder if you try to handle it all alone. If there is ever to be a time in your life when you need help, this is that time. You need to think right away about looking for someone to support you. Reach out in any constructive way you can—by telling your parents you have been reading this book, by showing up at the dinner table with the tears still on your face, by making an appointment with your school counselor. Don't wait, as some children of cancer patients do, until you are in serious emotional trouble—stealing or taking drugs or failing in school as a signal that you need help with your pain. And beware of falling into the trap of thinking that needing support is weakness, or that you have no right to upset your parents with your own concerns at this time of crisis. You have every right. In fact, your parents may be waiting for you to share what is on your mind so that they can help you.

Reach out to your parents first, because open communication will make the weeks ahead easier for everyone within your family. Reach out even if you are sure your parents won't listen or understand, even if you've tried talking to your mother or father before and it didn't work. This time could be different. If your parents don't respond, perhaps it is it because they they are too frightened, or too busy, or too out of practice at communicating to hear you right now. Try again, though. Maybe they will respond later.

It is inevitable, however, that some parents will not be able to communicate with their children—now or in the future. "I've tried talking to Dad," says Joan, "but I don't think he really wants to hear about it. The only thing he'll say to me is you have to go on, and that's the extent of his conversation." Lorna remembers when her mother first got sick: "For those first three months Dad's whole life centered around trying to get her well and finding out everything he could, and he was running himself ragged and everything, and he just wasn't interested in us." George's mother yelled at him when he tried to talk to her and told him to stop being so selfish and to start thinking about others in the family for a change.

If Your Parents Don't Respond

What do you do if your parents don't respond? You need to find someone else to talk to—a relative, an older friend, a doctor, a school friend, a teacher, a coach, a psychiatrist or psychologist, a school counselor, a social worker at the hospital, a neighbor, someone at a Crisis Center. Probably over the years you've read other books and pamphlets that refer you to a minister or a school counselor for one reason or another, and you've always said, "That's not for me." Try to get past that. You *need* someone to talk to. Listen to the words of other children of cancer patients who have been there and know what it's like:

> If you don't have a friend you can talk to, then go out and find someone...
>
> It's a bad situation but if you can talk about it, get it out in the open, you can live with it, it's something you can deal with...
>
> I wish I had had someone even just to listen to me—not so much to understand, but just so I could get it out. It would have helped so much.
>
> I really didn't have anyone to talk to. I think that's why, after...[my father's] death, I took it so hard, because I had all this pent up inside and no one to turn to...

One of the hardest parts of having a loved one ill with cancer is that you feel powerless much of the time. Finding someone you can talk to about your feelings is one constructive thing you can do. Some of you will know right away who will be a good person for that role. Others will have to be more creative, more aggressive, more cour-ageous about finding someone.

How Do You Find Help?

Suppose you've tried to talk to your parents about what is going on in your family and are not getting anywhere. Suppose also that you don't have any adult friend or relative with whom you are comfortable. But you are feeling pretty bad about things at the moment and know you need help. What is the first step you take?

If you are in school, you might start by going to your

guidance counselor, even if you have always thought of him or her as a specialist in helping people decide about colleges or jobs. If the counselor doesn't have a lot of experience with your particular concerns, or if he doesn't have time to give you the kind of extended personal attention he feels you need, he can refer you to someone who does. He might suggest, for example, that you contact a cancer care agency, or a mental health clinic, or another more specialized agency. For instance, if you are worried that your caregiving parent is becoming alcohol-dependent, he might suggest that you call Alateen, which is a support group for children of alcoholics (see Chapter 5). The counselor might make a phone call and set up an appointment for you to talk to someone at one of these agencies, or he might give you a phone number and suggest that you make an appointment on your own.

It may seem hard, after you have summoned up the courage to contact the guidance counselor in the first place, to be given only a phone number for your trouble. But it is important not to give up at this point. Try to make the call right away, before you get distracted, or lose your courage, or even lose the number. And when you call, keep in mind that agencies—even helping agencies—are not always very efficient, and you may get a busy signal or be put on hold for what seems like a long time. Or the person who answers may be a receptionist who is rushed or impersonal or whose voice just rubs you the wrong way. But just say to that person, "I am having some problems because my mother (or father) has cancer, and I want to make an appointment to come in and talk about it." You don't have to like the person who answers the phone—you will probably be seeing someone else. All you need to do now is to make an appointment to talk to someone at a later date. (Keep in mind also that at some agencies you may have to see an Intake worker when you first arrive, someone who will then decide who is the best person within the agency to help you.) If this sounds like a lot of trouble, you need to remember that it is for a very good cause—finding you a support person, giving you an outlet for the feelings that are building up inside you, making you feel better about what is going on in your family and your life.

If you are not in school, or if your school does not have a guidance counselor, you might need to find an appropriate helping agency yourself. Look in the white pages of your phone book under "Cancer" or "Mental Health." Or perhaps call the local Community Chest to find out what agencies might best help you with your particular problem. In some communities the phone book has a page that lists health care and community resources. Or call 1–800–4–CANCER (National Cancer Institute)[1] for further suggestions. There are many ways to get started, but remember that you may have to make more than one phone call before you find the help you need. Sit down at the phone and make a pact with yourself that you will not get up until you have actually made an appointment with someone who can help you. If you don't get help at one number, ask the person you talk to where else you might call. And when you finally have an appointment made, write it down on your calendar so that you won't forget to go.

Why Do You Need Someone?

Why is it so important to communicate at this time? In some cases you may *need* outside help with your problems. The stress in your family produced by illness may cause

---

[1] See p. 12 for the NCI numbers to call if you live in Washington, D.C., Alaska, or Hawaii.

one or both of your parents to drink excessively or to become abusive toward you or your brothers or sisters. (See Chapter 5 for further discussion of these issues.) In other cases, having someone to talk to is less critical but still important because it will make you feel better. Perhaps, as some children do, you find yourself wishing that it was the sick parent who was well and the other parent who had gotten sick. An outside person can help you get perspective on such problems, make you feel less guilty (such thoughts are perfectly normal), give you information, back you up when you need extra support.

Talking helps to lighten the burden of feelings, just as crying does. It can be a wonderful tension-reliever. You can get a different outlook on your feelings and fears just in the act of putting them into words in the presence of a listener. Discussing your problems can also help you to feel less as though they were out of control.

At one support group meeting, several members shared deep-rooted feelings of guilt and responsibility about their parents' illnesses. Latoya had been the only one at home with her sick father when he started having breathing problems. She had wanted to call an ambulance right away, but her father didn't want to go back to the hospital, and every time she mentioned the ambulance he started crying. Finally she did call, but when her father died several days later she couldn't shake off the feeling that her delaying had been the cause of her father's death.

Rosanne told a similar story. Feeling helpless and frustrated about her father's illness, she had tried to find something to do to help him. "I really got upset at the nurse," she remembered, "and I said, 'Tell me, what can I do, I've really got to do something,' and finally she said, 'Well, you can bring him his nutrient in some milk,' and when he drank that he stopped breathing, and that started me thinking that if I hadn't brought him that stuff he might still have been able to breathe. And I think about that a lot."

Ryan had read that some people believe stress can cause cancer. He wondered if his parents' concern about the asthma he had had when he was a child had caused his dad's tumor to develop. Ryan knew intellectually that he probably wasn't responsible for his dad's condition, but it wasn't until he had voiced his fears that he started to feel his worry lighten. Latoya and Rosanne had the same reaction. After telling their stories they also felt relieved, freer. Interestingly, with all three of the members, it didn't even require someone's saying to them, "Of course you're not really to blame!" to make them feel better. Just voicing their feelings in a sympathetic environment was enough.

Other people need more active help with their feelings. Lonnie actively hated his father and since the age of fourteen had been counting the days until he could leave home for good. When his father died from liver cancer, Lonnie felt triumphant at first, but then he became severely depressed. He needed psychiatric help to understand that having wished his father dead so many times, he now felt guilty. In fact, Lonnie discovered that he had been feeling personally responsible for his father's death from cancer.

Probably you know that children aren't responsible for their parents' health; that angry feelings can't cause someone's death, or good behavior a recovery; that if someone as ill as Latoya's father or Rosanne's father dies it is the cancer that kills him rather than anything a family member does or says. But you might need occasionally to be reminded of what you already know. Having someone to talk to at such times is important not only because it allows you to get your feelings out, but also because it gives you the opportunity to have information and insights—and reassurance—come in.

You will undoubtedly have lots of questions about your parent's cancer and your own feelings in the weeks and months ahead. It will be easier to ask for help when the time comes if you establish connections now with someone who will be there for you when needed. For some of you, that will be a person with whom you already have a relationship; for others, a new relationship, perhaps with a professional counselor, will seem to offer you more space to be truly honest about what you are going through. You need to think about what kind of relationship will make you feel most comfortable. In any case, look for a person who is not judgmental, who will understand that you have a right to whatever feelings you are feeling. No feeling you are experiencing is silly or bad. No feeling is unworthy of you.

Why Friends May Not Be Helpful

Can friends ever fill this supportive role? In the past your friends at school were probably the ones who listened to your complaints about your parents and encouraged you as you dealt with various problems. Some of those friends may still be there to help as you deal with your parent's cancer. But many children of cancer patients have found friends to be less than helpful at this particular time. Having a parent who has cancer, who ultimately even may die of cancer, makes you different from your peers. Your whole life is changing, your priorities are going to change. While you are worrying about losing a parent and about your family finances and about whether you are going to be able to pursue your life plans, your friends are focused on concerns that may seem trivial to you now. It is not their fault: There is nothing wrong with them *or* you. It is just that your lives have taken different paths.

Some teenage children of cancer patients are uncomfortable because they feel on display; they sense that others at school are looking at them, watching them to see how they are reacting. Nelson felt so embarrassed by the conspicuousness of his situation at school that when he went to camp for the summer he kept his mother's illness a secret. He felt guilty and disloyal to his mother for doing so, but actually his embarrassment was a perfectly natural reaction under the circumstances. Some of that kind of embarrassment fades with experience, with getting used to the fact of your parent's illness. And most people at school pay a lot less attention to your situation than you think.

Be aware also that just as cancer frightens you, it will frighten your friends. Some good friends may shy away from you because they don't know what to say to you. Seventeen-year-old Bonnie explains her friends' withdrawal this way: "I think they were uncomfortable because I knew what was going on, I knew that things weren't looking good, and I'd express that, and then they wouldn't know how to react. I think they were afraid that they'd say the wrong thing and get me all upset, and they didn't want that." The idea of a parent's dying may be so terrifying to some of your friends that they are uncomfortable being with you, with someone who reminds them that something like that could also happen in their family. One result is that they cut off your attempts to talk about what is really on your mind. Time and again group members referred to this experience:

> Your friends, oh, sure, they'll listen and everything, but then they'll say—like, don't worry about it, I'm sure everything will be okay—and I'm sitting there

trying to tell them it doesn't look good, I don't think she's going to get better, but they just kept giving me this false hope. They probably didn't want to deal with it any more than I did...

I told my friends my dad had cancer and they changed the subject like it was no big deal—I don't know if they knew how bad it could be or what...

I tried to talk to my boyfriend one night and he wouldn't even talk about it. I mean, you know, he just kind of ignored that I talked to him and he said, this isn't the time or place for something like that. Which was kind of rough.

Group members also felt very angry at friends who said to them, "I know how you feel." "My friends would always come up to me and go..., 'Oh, I know exactly how you feel,'" says sixteen-year-old Doris, "and they really *don't*, because they expected me to just jump in and be happy and forget about everything else, and that was really hard." Doris felt isolated and put off by such statements, even though she knew her friends were only trying to help.

Other kinds of difficulties arise with friends, too. "Even in the summertime I can't always do what I want," explains Lucy. "And if I tell my friends I have to cut the grass or do something like that they don't understand why someone else can't do it. I have to pick up responsibilities at home that they don't have to, and they just don't understand." Ron doesn't bring his friends home because he hates having to tell them to be quiet. His father is having a difficult time with chemotherapy right now, and noise often bothers him. Shannon is acutely aware that her house smells of illness. Elise knows that while she visits with her friends she has to watch her little brother, too.

Some children of cancer patients, faced with problems like these, choose instead to do all their socializing outside their home. Whenever possible they opt to go to a friend's house or a movie instead of inviting someone home. Sometimes, especially if the person has a good friend who is understanding and whose parents are understanding, this can work out very well, even providing a refuge at times when problems get too heavy at home. But other teens feel uncomfortable not being able to reciprocate and eventually stop accepting invitations or even cut themselves off from friendships so that the invitations do not come.

You might try instead to find ways in which you *can* entertain your friends. Try to think of times when your sick parent normally feels his best, or when someone else will be available to take over the caregiver role and give you some uninterrupted socializing time. Maybe you can work out a schedule with brothers or sisters so that each of you has some time-off you can count on. Maybe you can fix up some basement or garage space where noise won't bother anyone. Or you can have friends over for an outdoor activity like a picnic or a badminton game. It's worth some creative thinking to try to stay in touch with friends, because friends are important to provide you with a break from dealing with illness. As was said earlier, everyone suffering a loss needs to grieve, but no one needs to grieve all the time.

Sometimes special problems arise with friends of the opposite sex. All the disappointments and resentments at having to adjust your plans to the family's needs may seem multiplied when it comes to having to turn down a date with someone you really like. It can be particularly painful when a boyfriend or girlfriend is not able to meet your needs or help you deal with your problems. Breaking up with a boyfriend or a girlfriend in whom you have invested much emotion hurts a lot under ordinary circumstances, but the pain can seem almost unbearable when you are already emotionally vulnerable. Your pain can be eased by sharing it with someone who will let you talk and cry about it. And don't forget—the person you go to for support should also be available to share happiness with you. Life will not consist only of problems from now on. There will be joys and triumphs you will want to celebrate.

Making Contact with Teens with Similar Problems

This is not to say that some friends won't be there for you, won't rise to the occasion and help you through this difficult time. But even a best friend can get tired of dealing continually with heavy problems. Your need to talk will remain, however, and sometimes you will need to talk about the same problems again and again. One group of your contemporaries who can be helpful at this point is other teenagers who themselves have been through the serious illness and death of a parent. Although you may think at times that you are the only one unlucky enough to have this burden placed on you, there are many other children of cancer patients who are feeling much the same way. Sharing feelings with them can be a great relief to you all.

If your mother or father is receiving treatment at a hospital, the hospital social worker or chaplain would probably be the best person to help you make contact with other children of seriously ill parents. Your school counselor may be able to help you find someone. If there are support groups in your area (again, ask at the hospital or phone the cancer agencies in your city[2]), these can be very useful to you at this time. "If at all possible," advises eighteen-year-old Teri, "try to get involved with a group. I know a lot of people are scared to get involved and they think, 'I don't want to go, I don't want to share,' but everybody's in the same situation and it's so much help."

A support group allows people with similar problems to get together to let out their feelings, to share experiences, and to help one another. A support group for teenage children of cancer patients allows them to get together to talk regularly, with the help of a trained adult leader. In group you can talk freely about issues that really matter to you with people who want and need to hear about what you're going through. "When I tried to discuss something at home with my sisters," complained Joellen, "they would say, 'She's so morbid!'—that's what they called it—and then I would say to myself, 'Okay, be that way!' and I would go into the other room and then they would say, 'She gets so *upset!*' But that wasn't the case. They were just telling me that they didn't want to listen."

Jennie's mother was willing to listen, but in trying to make Jennie feel better she seemed to be putting limits on the emotion Jennie could display. "Mom says that because I've always taken things so hard," says Jennie, "that I'm looking for—not pity—but I just get carried away, I take things too far. I just get upset easier than everybody else, that's all. And I thought there was something wrong with me. But in group it feels good to be able to be around people that understand. When I walked in here I thought,

---

[2] If the agencies or professionals in your area are not familiar with how cancer support groups for teenagers work, they can contact Cancer Family Care, Inc. of Cincinnati, 7710 Reading Road, Cincinnnati, OH 45237.

'I'm going to be the only one in here that's like that,' but it wasn't that way."

People in group don't get tired of hearing about your problems; they have similar problems, and they know that they need to talk, too. And hearing you talk about your problems helps them. If you feel sometimes that you wish your sick parent would die and get it over with (people do feel that; it is a normal reaction to a long and wearing illness), then they feel less guilty feeling that way also. Ideally, being in group gives all members the same opportunity to test out and vent their feelings, to break down the feeling of isolation that their parent's illness may have thrust upon them. Cara and her brother Donald were in a group together. Until that time they had never talked to each other about their fears over how their father was handling their mother's illness, about their resentment at not being given adequate information about her condition. Each had been feeling scared and lonely all alone. After group was under way for a few weeks, they were able to communicate at home and be supportive to each other. Often group members exchange phone numbers, call each other at particular stressful times between meetings, ultimately become friends.

You may still feel funny about getting involved with a group, especially if you haven't had much experience with such things. Some people think that support groups are for people with "real" problems, teens on drugs or alcohol, people who are mentally ill or emotionally disturbed. You may even feel that to seek out a group would be to set yourself apart, to say that something is wrong with you. But on the contrary, joining a group doesn't set you apart—it brings you together with people just like you.

The fact is that cancer changes lives. As perhaps you have experienced already, cancer in a family can change family relationships rapidly and turn everything in your life upside down. It can make the people you usually turn to for support inaccessible, require you to act like an adult before you're ready, make people treat you like a child when you feel you're ready for honesty and responsibility, turn economically secure families into struggling ones. It can make you feel confused, angry, resentful, even crazy sometimes. There is nothing wrong with a person who looks for help under those circumstances. In fact, looking for help, finding someone to talk to is a sign of strength. As Teri says, "Don't be scared. It's just going to help you."

CHAPTER 5

Taking Care of Your Own Health

C oping with cancer in your family is hard work. It is important that you try to keep fit, emotionally and physically, so that you can deal with whatever you will have to face in the weeks and months ahead. There is a very real connection between emotional stress and physical symptoms, and many children of cancer patients find themselves losing weight, gaining weight, feeling exhausted, having headaches, skipping menstrual periods as a result of the tension surrounding them. Other physical symptoms of emotional distress include hyperactivity, sleep disturbances, hyperventilation, rashes, constant colds, nausea, feelings of dizziness or disorientation, and pain in various parts of the body. If you are not feeling well, arrange a visit to your doctor. He or she should be able to help you in a number of ways.

Will You Get Cancer, Too?

One important way that a doctor can help you is by assuring you that you are not getting cancer yourself. It is not at all unusual if you are living with and worrying about cancer all the time to start thinking that you might be getting it too, even though it is statistically very unlikely that you would get cancer at the same time as your parent. After all, cancer isn't contagious, and it isn't a disease that many children get. But if you still feel uneasy about certain symptoms, don't hesitate to discuss them with your doctor or school nurse. A medically trained person can determine the cause of the symptoms and help you with treatment, whatever the cause may be.

Many close relatives of cancer patients also worry that they will get cancer in the future. They know that cancer has a hereditary factor that is not completely understood. It is true that certain kinds of cancer (not all cancers) do sometimes run in families, but that does not mean that if your parent has one of those cancers you will *necessarily* get cancer some day. It means only that your chances of getting the disease eventually are *somewhat greater* than those of the average population. Perhaps when you are an adult you may need to have more frequent medical checkups. Here again, it would be wise to talk to your doctor or your parent's doctor about the specific kind of cancer your parent has. Get some good, solid information. Remember that cancer is a group of more than one hundred diseases, so it is important to ask about your parent's individual case. And keep asking until you get full information; anything less may cause you to worry unnecessarily.

Are You Going Crazy?

Many children of cancer patients worry also about their own mental state. Lila is upset at how unstable her emotions seem: "I'm okay and then some little something's said and I'll be crying. I don't *like* it." Jeff loses his temper and keeps shouting at people in a way he never did before his father got sick. He doesn't seem to be able to control himself, even though he's been sent to the principal's office twice in the past week. Mark, on the other hand, feels numb all the time, as if there is a sad buzzing in his head. Since his mother went into the hospital this last time he has been finding it hard to concentrate in school; some days he doesn't even bother to go at all. He can't summon up energy for basketball practice either, and since none of his friends come by anymore, he spends most of his afternoons alone just wandering the streets until dinner. He knows people think he is being weird, but he doesn't seem to be able to act any other way. He would go see the school counselor but he's afraid that the counselor will tell him he's really flipping out, and he doesn't know what he would do then.

All of these young people—in different ways and to different degrees—are showing stress reactions. Their reactions do not mean that they are mentally ill or abnormal in any way. All of them were experiencing very strong feelings of pain and fear and anger about their parent's illness, and such feelings, if not given expression naturally, often make their appearance in other ways—for example, in Jeff's problem behavior at school, in Lila's frequent tears, in Mark's numbness and depression. The feeling of being out of control or going crazy is one that many children of cancer patients experience, and it is one they all find very frightening. Learning that others in the same situation feel the same way can be a first step in alleviating that fear. As one group member summed it up wryly: "You know what? I think I've just learned that weird is normal under the circumstances."

When Should You Seek Professional Help?

Jeff and Lila and Mark all could have benefited from seeking help with their feelings, because such help might have eliminated the symptoms that were interfering with their daily lives and causing them additional pain. It might be argued that help was not absolutely necessary, and, in fact, that all three might have found their way through their pain on their own, because all were basically healthy people. But there is enough unavoidable pain involved in having a parent sick with cancer without having to add unnecessary pain to the equation. Why is it that people will readily go to a doctor for a sore foot but don't consider it equally justifiable to seek professional help for emotional distress? Emotional pain is equally real and sometimes hurts even more than physical pain. And like physical pain, if treated when it first begins, it is likely to go away faster and more easily than if you wait until it immobilizes you.

Some emotional ailments *should* be checked out by a doctor. It is normal to feel depressed about a parent's serious illness or death, but normal depression is temporary—even though at the time it may *seem* to go on forever. If the depression doesn't lighten with time, or if it begins to cause serious problems with day-to-day functioning, the depressed person should be seen by a doctor. Depression is a word that is often used to mean sadness, but the illness that is termed "clinical depression" is described often as a lack of feeling. Nothing seems worthwhile. Even happy experiences do not produce pleasure. A person may act bored and uninterested, mope around the house, tire easily, feel worthless, stop caring about personal appearance. Or a person may act out the feeling that nothing matters by becoming wild and unruly, by getting into various kinds of trouble such as shoplifting or stealing cars. Sometimes depression is related to accepting blame for something you didn't do, as in the case of Lonnie in Chapter 4, who felt that his hostile thoughts and his desire for independence had caused his father to die. Sometimes it is caused by a chemical imbalance in the body and can be relieved with appropriate medication. Another definition of depression is "anger turned inward." But in any case, continuing depression should be taken seriously, because it can and sometimes does lead to suicide. It is difficult to recognize such depression in yourself, but *if you do have concerns about your emotional state, if you are thinking about suicide, if someone else is concerned about you and suggests that you seek help, or if you are worried about the mental state of someone in your family, talk to a trusted adult immediately. Or consult a doctor or a professional counselor or call a suicide hotline right away. You have nothing to lose.*

As you have probably guessed from the above, it is not easy to tell one kind of depression from another unless you are trained to do so. Likewise it is not always easy to distinguish other "normal" symptoms of grief and stress from those that are too intense or last too long or are likely to put the well-being of the grieving person in jeopardy. Doctors and other professionals, however, who have seen many patients or clients go through the various stages of grieving, are in a position to tell the difference. They will not judge you or scold you for making too big a deal about feeling bad. Don't hesitate to use their services if you are worried or feel you need help. And don't wait until you feel terrible. Under circumstances like this, it is never too soon to look for help.

Looking for Comfort

People who are upset or who are suffering loss need comfort. It is healthy to seek comfort in a healthy way, but many teenage children of cancer patients fail to see that their emotional neediness puts them at risk at this particular time. It is important for you to consider especially carefully the intimate relationships you get involved in. It can be very tempting to go for something that feels good at a time when everything else in your life feels so bad. But if you take some moments to think ahead about where you want your relationships to go, you will be less likely to let the combination of a strong sex drive and an equally strong need for comfort push aside your warning voices and cause you additional anguish in the long run.

You need comfort, but you don't need additional problems. Sex, under the right circumstances, when the partners are emotionally ready and are able to take on the responsibilities involved, can be truly beautiful. But used for the wrong reasons, at the wrong time in your life, it can have consequences that can permanently damage your life.

Sexually Transmitted Diseases

What are those consequences? First of all is the risk of sexually transmitted diseases (STDs), including AIDS. AIDS is now known to be transmitted heterosexually, through intimate contact between persons of opposite sexes, as well as by homosexual relationships. The teenage population is thought to be the next group at major risk of contracting AIDS. If a person you have sexual relations with is an intravenous drug user or has previously had sexual relations with a person having AIDS, you too are at risk of contracting this fatal disease. For that reason, if you are thinking about entering into a sexual relationship with someone, you have no choice but to take into consideration all the people with whom your partner may have had relations in the past. With the chance of contracting AIDS always a real possibility, any sexual encounter nowadays means trusting your partner—literally—with your life.

Other sexually transmitted diseases carry serious emotional and physical risks as well. Genital herpes, gonorrhea, syphilis, and chlamydia, for example, can all cause short-term emotional and physical distress and serious long-term health problems. These diseases can affect a woman's future ability to have children. Should pregnancy occur, they can also affect the health of her newborn baby.

Pregnancy

Another possible long-term consequence of sexual relationships is pregnancy. Even with protection, pregnancy is always a risk in sexual intercourse. Some teens who want to be loved, who feel left out, who need to be comforted and to have someone care about them, actually think that having a baby will fill their needs, without understanding that babies are takers, not givers. As a teenage child of a cancer patient, you are probably already weighed down by extra household duties, responsibilities, and worries that seem too burdensome for your years. A baby would just add to that burden and would remain your constant responsibility for eighteen years to come. Those of you, on the other hand, who conceive and decide that you are not able to keep the baby are faced with loss, a real and serious loss that is often accompanied by its own full-fledged grief reaction. The father as well as the mother of the baby experiences this loss. Along with the grief that you are already feeling about your sick parent, this new grief would add up to a terrible psychological burden for you to bear.

One teen suggested that you think of it this way: Your parent is fighting his illness right now, fighting to preserve his life, battling for his future. Your present life has been disrupted by the cancer, too, but you also need to try to preserve *your* future. You want to be able to go into that future with all the options you can, in good health, unburdened by a child, free to go to college or travel or pursue a chosen trade or career. Your turn has been delayed, but it will come. When it does, don't you want to be able to make the best of it?

Clarifying Your Goals

Again, the best advice is that you sit down and think very hard about your goals, your values, and what you want to do with your life, both short term and in the future. You might use a problem-solving technique such as the following. First, clarify the problem. Is the problem that you are afraid John will dump you if you don't have sex with him? or that you feel miserable and lonely and want someone of your own to pay attention to you? or that you're tired of feeling like The Person With The Problem and just want to be normal and have a good time for a change? or that you don't know how to say no to John when he comes over every afternoon after school and your parents are never home? Is it that you're angry at your parents for neglecting you and want to do something to make them sit up and take notice? or that you really love John and want to express your love sexually even though everyone tells you you're too young? or that you feel illness all around you and want to do something to make yourself feel really alive? Or what?

Once you have pinpointed the problem, your second step is to think of alternative solutions. Let your mind run free and think of as many solutions as possible, even if they don't seem entirely realistic. Third, list the pros and cons (think about consequences here) for each possible solution. Fourth, decide which solution makes the most sense to you. Base your decision on the pros and cons you have listed. And fifth, act on your decision.

Problem-solving according to that model can be useful in a number of ways. It takes some time to do, but decisions having consequences that can affect your entire life deserve that kind of consideration—you don't want to make such decisions impulsively in the back seat of a car.

You may discover some interesting things in the process of doing this kind of thinking. For instance, you may find that sex is frequently used to try to solve problems that are not really sexual. Teenagers—both male and female—use sex to make their parents angry, to get their own way, to fill a void in their lives, to be popular, because they can't think of a way out. Sometimes, obviously, it is also used to meet sexual needs, but even in those cases the point should be made that many stages of intimacy short of intercourse can meet sexual needs—and without the life-disrupting consequences that can result from having intercourse at this stage of your life. For example, many teens (and other people) masturbate as a way of relieving sexual tension; if doing so falls within your value system it is a perfectly acceptable thing to do. You certainly need not feel guilty about it, nor should you feel guilty about experiencing sexual pleasure of any kind because your parent is sick. Positive feelings, including pleasure, are to be valued at a time when there seems to be a constant ache in your life, when so many things about your existence are sad or problematical. The thing to ask, however, is whether any "quick fix" of gratification is likely to have long-term consequences and bring you far greater pain in the long run.

If, after careful consideration of the consequences and despite the advice of experts and many teenage parents ("I should have waited," is the cry often heard at counseling centers), you decide to become active sexually, at least be aware of various forms of protection available. Two essential considerations are contraception and safe sex. If pregnancy or an STD should result from your sexual activity, don't try to hide or ignore the problem or solve it alone. See your doctor or a counseling agency such as Planned Parenthood right away for responsible medical information and help with decision-making. STDs and pregnancy are not problems that can be expected to go away on their own.

Sexual Abuse

At this time when you are so emotionally vulnerable, you should be aware of another danger area. Teenage girls in particular should know that the potential for sexual abuse exists in a situation where a mother is sick or hospitalized for a long time, the father is depressed and frustrated, and the teenage daughter is cast in the role of the mother or wife substitute. Taking on the responsibility for keeping the household running should *never* be interpreted as including an obligation to fill the sexual role of your absent parent. You can meet your responsibility in this case *only* by saying no and immediately getting the help of another adult, never by giving in to your parent's request. Your parent may be confused and hurting badly, but you are not the right person to comfort him in this way. Sexual comfort from a child can never make a parent feel better in the long run; it can only do further and possibly permanent damage to your family and all its members.

Incest and sexual abuse are very difficult subjects, and some adults you try to discuss them with may brush off your concerns and appear not to be taking your fears seriously. People often deny a problem beause they can't bring themselves even to think about something they consider so terrible. *You, however, should not give up your search for help and protection,* because you need support and probably professional advice to handle this kind of problem. You might start by talking to a relative, preferably an adult who is not living in the household. If that person is not helpful, try talking to your doctor, or your clergyperson, or a teacher, or a school counselor. If you feel uncomfortable talking with someone you know, you might start by calling 1–800–422–4453, the Childhelp USA national hotline. That number is answered twenty-four hours a day, and the person who answers your call will be able to counsel you and to refer you to someone in your area who can help you. You should be advised, however, that helping agencies sometimes move slowly, and you must try not to be discouraged if you don't get the help you want immediately. *Keep trying.*

You also need to know that once official wheels start turning on your charge of sexual abuse, the situation in your family may get worse before it gets better. Your parents may be very angry at you for seeking outside help. You will be interviewed about your experience, and you may be tempted at that time to back off and not to tell the truth about what happened. But it is impc ant that you realize how essential it is for both you and your family that you get help. In most cases parents who abuse don't want to hurt their children, but they just can't stop on their own. Often they need outside pressure to force them to get the help they need.

Remember also that even if you have already given in to your parent's sexual demands, *you still deserve help.* You are not to blame, and you need not feel guilty about what has happened to you. You are a victim. There are people in the community who will understand this and will reach out without judgment to help you, but you need to let them know you need help. Don't delay, and keep asking until you get the help you need.

Other Concerns

Several other issues regarding sexuality need to be mentioned here. Some teens worry that because their parent has cancer, they themselves will be unable to have children. There is no connection at all between a parent's cancer and a teenager's ability to bear children. Your ability some day to have a family will not be affected.

Other teenage children of cancer patients worry that their ill parent will pass the cancer to their well parent through sexual relations, and they are frightened or offended at the idea that their parents might still be sexually intimate despite the seriousness of the illness. First of all, remember that cancer is *not* contagious. The fact that your parents can still be intimate is not a danger to anyone. Rather, it can be a great comfort, something to sustain them through this difficult time, a demonstration of the love that brought them together and brought you into the world. But not all marital partners benefit from this closeness. Sometimes the parent without cancer worries about hurting a sick partner or imposing on him or her. Sometimes a husband or wife worries whether sexual intimacy is appropriate, is the right thing to do. Although this is a personal decision, a matter of individual feelings, it is worth knowing (and possibly finding a way to share this information with your parents) that it is certainly not wrong for marital partners to continue sexual intimacy if they wish to do so. Many cancer patients speak of this closeness as a great comfort, a great pleasure in their otherwise troubled lives. They know also that sex is more than the act of intercourse—it is holding, and loving, and sharing. It is a life force, when a life force is needed.

Drugs and Alcohol

In any time of great stress and painful feelings, it is hard to believe that the pain and stress will ever go away. The temptation is great to try to escape, to avoid your problems and your anguish through use of drugs or alcohol. All kinds of chemical substances hold potential for abuse. That includes medication a doctor might prescribe to help you relax and get to sleep, the alcohol that adults seem to use to get through their stressful days, or hard drugs that you find at school or on the street. All the warnings you've received that drug use is addictive, destructive, possibly fatal in the long run may seem pale compared to the pain you are feeling. If this pain is going to go on and on, you say to yourself, why not take a chance and go into a drug-numbed haze until it is all over one way or the other?

The answer is that when it comes to grief, drug use is a solution that *simply does not work*. Aside from the usual arguments against abuse of chemical substances, you have to be forewarned that you would be applying a solution that runs counter to everything that is known about grief work. Think about what you read in Chapter 3 about mourning or grieving. Virtually all experts agree that you need to *pass through* the pain, to feel it, in order to be free of it. The work of grieving has to be done in order to recover. If you dull your feelings constantly with drugs or alcohol, you are preventing yourself from facing the grief and getting it out. And if the grief is not worked through, it will almost certainly cause you other, more serious problems later in life.

If you do have chemical dependency problems and decide you need help, you can call Alcoholics Anonymous or the National Council on Alcoholism chapter in your area. See the phone book for their numbers. The National Council on Alcoholism should be a good source of information on drug programs in your area as well as alcohol programs. Teachers in your school and your school counselor should also be able to direct you to agencies that can help you with your dependency problem.

Your Parents' Problems and Problems with Your Parents

Your parents' grief and how they handle it can cause you additional stress. Many parents under normal circumstances do not let their children see that they are vulnerable to fear and despair, and seeing a parent break down can be very frightening to a child who has had no previous experience with adult grief. You may worry not only about your sick parent but also about your other parent who is wavering under the additional load of caregiving and financial responsibilities. You may be concerned that your well parent is making himself sick with anxiety and crying and think that if you weren't around he would have that much less to worry about. ("Can't you behave?" your parent shouts. "With all I have to contend with, do I have to worry about you, too?") You may even be worried that he will develop some fatal illness or commit suicide and then you will have no one. If you are seriously worried, talk to an adult friend or relative to relieve your concerns and to try to help you persuade your parent to get the support he or she needs. Remember, though, that your parents need to express their own grief, too. They are probably just as sad and confused as you are, and some of what you see may be their way of working out those feelings.

Several other areas having to do with your parents' behavior should be mentioned here because of the effect they can have on your own physical and mental health. Some parents, instead of turning to their own friends and other adults, become overdependent on their children for company and emotional support. They may tell you personal things you don't feel comfortable hearing or expect you to give up all your own activities to be with them. Such a situation is not healthy for either you or your parent. Certainly you need sometimes to offer help or comfort, but it is also important for you to keep at least part of your life as normal as possible. You are your parent's child, not her therapist or his best buddy. Your parents are still the head of the family and will be better off if they are expected to act as such. And you are still a child, even though you may be expected to take on some adult responsibilities. Often it takes a neutral third party—a hospital social worker, a clergyperson, a caring relative, a family therapist—to help family members see what illness has done to mix up their roles. But it is healthier for the whole family when everyone gets back in the role where he or she belongs.

When You Need Protection

As mentioned earlier, sometimes this mix-up of roles in a family can also result in sexual abuse—when a child is expected to meet the sexual needs of a parent (see pp. 70–72). No one should ever feel that he or she has to meet these needs of a parent.

Other kinds of parental abuse can also result from serious illness in a family. The stress of cancer can cause even caring parents to become physically or emotionally abusive. Or the parent who is sick and in the hospital may be the one who protected the children from abuse by the other parent. Extreme neglect of children is also a form of abuse. Any child suffering abuse deserves help and should seek it immediately. (Call the Childhelp national hotline number, 1–800–422–4453, for assistance, or follow the other suggestions outlined in the section *Sexual Abuse*, pp. 70–72.) The fact that your mom or dad has cancer and may even be dying from it does not mean that you have to put up with abuse. You deserve better; you deserve to have someone on your side to help you, to protect you.

You may also need protection if your parents are abusing drugs or alcohol. (It should be made clear that cancer patients who take medically prescribed drugs for pain or other symptoms are not abusing the drugs when they use them properly for needed relief.) Both cancer patients and their spouses can be alcoholics or drug abusers. They may have been abusers before the diagnosis of cancer, or they may become abusers because they cannot deal in a mature way with the problems caused by the illness. As a child in such a family, you may feel helplessness and rage at seeing your already sick parent destroy himself by this other means. Your fears of being abandoned may be made worse by the knowledge that your remaining parent is drunk most of the time and not available to meet your legitimate needs. You may feel that you or your brothers or sisters are being put in danger emotionally and perhaps even physically by the substance abuse of your parent. You may even feel that your parent is killing himself.

In most cases, a good first step is to discuss your fears with your parent. But if your mother or dad won't admit to a chemical dependency problem, it may in the end be you who has to face up to it. Help is available for family members of alcoholics through Al-Anon (a support organization for all family members of alcoholics), or Alateen (specifically for teenage children of alcoholics). If there is no listing in your phone book under Al-Anon or Alateen, call the local chapter of the National Council on Alcoholism. Children of drug abusers may also call the National Council on Alcoholism for help in finding the right agency to assist them. Or look under the heading "Drugs" or "Health Care" or "Substance Abuse" in the community services listing of your white or yellow pages, and call any agency or hotline that sounds as if it might deal with your particular problem. Or call the social service department of any hospital that has a program for substance abusers. Tell the person who answers what your problem is, and ask for suggestions as to where you can get help.

The first steps are the hardest; those first phone calls may feel as if you're betraying your family. But help for the family of a substance abuser frequently is the beginning of life-saving help for the abuser. And help for him can save the family, too.

Taking Breaks from Illness

All the problems discussed in this chapter are heavy, serious problems. Perhaps you feel weighed down and depressed just reading about them. Living with any one of them can be even more draining. For that reason, it is essential for your health and well-being in this time of stress that you take breaks from illness. Those of you who have to give up participation in organized sports, as Walt did in Chapter 2, might want to make a point of running or working out on Nautilus—some physical activity that you can fit into your present illness-disrupted schedule. Physical activity is a great reliever of tension and is thought to act as an antidepressant. (Activities such as running also get you out of the house for a short time each day.) Being with friends (going to movies, playing pool, just fooling around), jobs, school activities, volunteer work, music, gardening, baby-sitting for children other than your younger brothers and sisters, weekend outings with another family, a week or a month at camp—anything that gives you a breather or a change of scene is likely to be beneficial.

"You have to take a break once in a while," says one seventeen-year-old child of a cancer patient. "You have to not deny reality but take a step back once in a while and not think about it every waking moment because otherwise it'll just eat you up." Sometimes it's hard to have a good time: "I'll feel my friends see I'm having fun," says Elizabeth, "and they think I've forgotten my dad and all that's happening, but they don't realize that nothing will ever be the same again. And lots of times I feel so guilty and I want them to know it still hurts." But most parents want their children to have fun; it is good, if you can, to step away from your troubles once in a while and do something nice for yourself. Having a good time is not being disloyal to your mom or dad; in fact, you will be setting a good example for them if you go out and try to enjoy yourself when the opportunity arises.

Facing Your Feelings

How do you feel right now? Depending on what stage of your parent's illness you are coping with, you may feel numb, or exhausted, or terrified, or in pretty good control of things. The point of this chapter is that you should try to keep yourself as strong and fit as you can in order to deal with whatever stresses the weeks ahead may bring. But keep in mind as you do that being strong means facing your feelings as they come up. It means being vulnerable to feelings. That goes for boys as well as girls—truly strong men have strong feelings and show them, despite what the popular "macho" message is on TV.

Sometimes the feelings may be frightening because they are confusing and contradictory, but that is because it is possible to think and feel many different things on many different levels all at the same time. You can love a person and still be angry that he needs so much attention; you can love him and resent the fact that your own needs are not being met; you can be sad about his illness and still have fun at a dance or a party. You can even love a person and wish he would die. But the feelings don't hurt him. Nothing you feel or hope or wish for in times of anger or despair (or any other time, for that matter) is by itself going to make anything happen.

Many people worry that anger or hate or resentment can backfire and actually make someone sick (or sicker). But they can't. Your feelings can't affect your parent's illness. In fact, the only real possibility of harm is to yourself if you don't acknowledge the feelings and let them out. Because feelings suppressed are feelings not disposed of—they are all too likely to show up disguised as physical symptoms or school failure or difficulty in forming relationships or unwanted pregnancy or chemical dependency. The trick is to acknowledge your feelings instead so that they can work for you in the process of healing. People who suffer a serious loss need to grieve—to feel—in order to be well.

CHAPTER 6

When Your Parent Is in the Hospital

"My dad was in the hospital for thirteen days last month," says Kerry, "and we went to visit him every day, and they really had him massively drugged up—and he just kind of sat there and looked at you—and you thought, is he going to be alive when I come back tomorrow? It really freaks you out. I hate hospitals. I mean, there were people all over coughing and I was, like, are they going to die in the bed next to him or what?"

"I know that death can happen anywhere," says Tony, "that you can be walking home and get hit by a car, but it brings it home when you're in a hospital. I hate going to hospitals."

Most people hate hospitals, no matter how nice or attractive the hospital, no matter how caring and welcoming the nursing staff. There is something about hospitals that makes people nervous—a sense that something mysterious is taking place, that death and suffering are going on and that eyes must be averted. People walk carefully and stiffly in hospitals. They tend to do what they are told. They defer to doctors and other medical staff as if they were gods and hesitate to challenge them or ask questions, although they have a perfect right to ask and be told what is going on.

Hospitals often become an important part in the life of a cancer patient and his family. The patient may go in for surgery, either at the time of diagnosis or later if the cancer progresses. He may go in for chemotherapy, or for radiation treatments, or for some other therapy. He may be admitted to stabilize a severe reaction to a particular treatment or because his doctors are afraid that there *will* be a severe reaction. From time to time he may go in for pain control. And eventually, should treatment fail, he may go into a hospital to die.

Not all admissions to a hospital mean that something momentous is happening in the course of a patient's illness. Admissions for some kinds of treatment are fairly routine. Patients may come into the hospital for a time, leave again, and go on with their lives; some may even get well. But even for those patients, some parts of their treatment may be extremely unpleasant and difficult for their families to witness. In movies and TV programs, patients in hospitals look like ordinary people—only in hospital gowns and perhaps with their hair mussed up. In real life patients may be bloated or vomiting or disoriented or hooked up to various tubes and machines. Sights and sounds and smells may be hard to take.

Not all patients go through the kinds of extreme disability described above. But some do. And you, as the child of a patient, need to know ahead of time what you have to face. You are used to having your parent be the strong one in the family. Seeing that parent in bed in the hospital can be a shock. Ross recalls taking one look at his mother in the Intensive Care Unit (ICU) and walking back out the door saying, "I can't go in. I absolutely cannot go in. I will not go in. I don't want to remember this."

Some people don't have that kind of reaction. But all do best if they are prepared, if they know what to expect. This chapter will help you to know what questions to ask so that you will be better prepared if you do have to visit your parent in the hospital. It will also give you some guidance on what to say and what to do.

Preparing Yourself for a Hospital Visit

The first thing you should do if you are going to visit in the hospital is to ask your well parent what kind of condition your sick parent is in. Have things changed noticeably since your parent was admitted to the hospital? What are the doctors doing? Are there any side effects you should be prepared for? Is your parent very weak? Will he or she feel like talking? Ask your well parent to be honest with you, not to sugarcoat the answers. And be aware that the changes resulting from certain medications can be rapid and startling. Your sick parent's face may be bloated so much in just a few days that you hardly recognize him. Hair loss can be sudden and may drastically change a person's appearance. IV tubes (intravenous tubes, which feed medications, nutrients, blood, or other fluids directly into a patient's veins) or catheters (which drain urine from a patient's body so that he doesn't have to get out of bed or use a bed pan to urinate) can be very upsetting to a visitor who is not used to seeing them. It helps to find out as much as possible about what is happening. Ask and try to get answers before you go.

You can also ask questions about *why* things are

happening. Some of the unpleasant reactions are the result of trade-offs: A medication that controls pain may make the patient disoriented and groggy; a medication that slows the growth of the cancer may cause mouth sores or swelling of the face. People often say to children simply: "The medication is helping your dad (or mom)." But what does helping mean? You may want to ask specifically—is it making him more comfortable, or will it help him get better? The more information you have, the better prepared you will be for what the future will bring. Ask also if the condition you see is temporary or permanent; you may be greatly comforted to know that certain conditions are side effects of a particular treatment and will disappear when that treatment has been completed.

When you go to the hospital and see your sick parent, you may be distressed because you think he or she must be in great pain. "I couldn't stand looking at Mom's arm," said Brandon. "It looked like it must kill her to have that needle in there. But when I asked her, she said that it hurt a little when they put it in, but it didn't hurt now at all." It is perfectly permissible to ask your parent if something hurts, or to ask if you can sit on the bed, or to ask if he or she is up to giving you a hug. But then another problem arises. What if you don't feel like giving your mom or dad a hug? What if the sights and smells in the hospital room make you want instead to back off, to run out of the room and take a deep breath somewhere?

Dealing with Your Own Discomfort

This can be a difficult problem, and it is certainly not a problem for children alone. Emotions run high in hospitals, and it is not unusual for someone to need time to be able to deal with certain situations. Asking for information and explanations is one way of dealing with the situation; for instance, it no longer upset Brandon to see his mother's IV after he knew it wasn't causing her any pain. Time-outs are also permissible. You can say to your parent, "I just need to take a walk; I'll be back," or even "I'll be back tomorrow." A little space may give you time to get used to what you are seeing or feeling. If you have trouble approaching your parent for a hug or a kiss, the bottom of the bed might seem safer; putting your hand on the bed and touching your parent's foot through the covers can also make a connection, can show your love and caring. Touch is important to a person who is very sick in the hospital because he probably doesn't feel very attractive, and that often means he doesn't feel lovable. Having his relatives want to be near him, to touch him, can give him reassurance that he is still loved.

Another alternative if you are having trouble dealing with a particular aspect of your parent's condition is to be as open and honest as Brandon was and say directly to your sick parent, "I have trouble looking at your IV (or colostomy, or amputation site) but I still love you. How do *you* deal with it? Does it bother you, too?" Far from offending your parent, you may be doing him a great service by giving him permission to talk about something that nobody else will talk to him about. And chances are you won't be as frightened about letting your feelings show the next time you walk into that room, because your parent will already know what bothers you. And you will know better what bothers him, too.

It is important to remember in situations such as this, however, that when you approach your parent honestly he may be angry or upset or start to cry. If that happens, keep in mind that it is not necessarily what you just said that your parent is upset about; a person sick with cancer is dealing with a lot, and your comment or question may simply be the trigger that allows him to release those feelings. If he cries or even gets angry, those are not necessarily bad reactions—they may actually be useful, honest ones. You can ask your parent: "Are you mad at me? Or are you mad because you're sick?" Sometimes people get angry at those they love and trust the most because those are the people they know will not desert them. Even though it can be hard to take anger from a sick parent, you can also feel special that you are the one to whom that release of feelings has been entrusted.

What Do You Talk About? What Do You Do?

What do you talk about when you go to visit someone in the hospital? What do you do? It can feel very awkward when you first go to the hospital; it may even seem as if your parent is a different person from the well parent you remember. But it is important to keep in mind that he or she is the same person—just as you are the same person you always were even though you find yourself visiting at a hospital.

Start with the idea that no matter how sick your parent is, he or she is still your parent, a parent who loves you and wants to be involved with your life. Share as you normally would the things that are going on in your life, problems included. Ask for advice if you need it, even about issues having to do with the illness. If your parent is in for a long hospital stay, you might want to bring in two dresses you are thinking of buying and ask your parent to help you decide which one to get. If you are on a school team, videotape a game and bring it in to watch together. Bring in report cards and school papers and stories about friends and dates. Or bring in cookies (ask the nurse first) from a

new recipe you've tried. A person in the hospital feels cut
off from the outside world. He doesn't want to be left out.
He wants to know what's going on with his family, even if
that means hearing about problems. He wants to feel
involved.

Sometimes other adults will caution you before you go
into a hospital room: "Smile now. Be cheerful. Don't let
her see you upset." But that kind of stiff-upper-lip attitude
cuts you off from your parent, makes your visit artificial.
You can let your sick parent know you're sad, if that's how
you are feeling; it will let her know you love her and may
even give her an opening to share her feelings with you. It
is also quite permissible—even desirable—to allow the
patient to comfort you. You can say, "I'm scared, I'm sad, I
could really use a hug. I really need you." That will make
your parent feel that she has not been written out of her
role as parent just because she is very ill right now. It will
make her feel valued, needed.

Some things are easier to say when you are alone with
your sick parent. But if you are too young to drive, you may
get to go to the hospital only when your other parent or
older brother or sister goes. There may be only one family
car. Because of school and work, everyone may have to go
together in the evening. But if you need to communicate
privately with your sick parent, it is important for you to
learn to say comfortably, "I would like to be alone with
Mom (or Dad) for half an hour." In fact, each family
member should be given the opportunity to visit alone
with the patient from time to time. Communication is
different when only two people are in a room talking
together. Or being quiet together. Because you should also
feel free to be silent with your sick parent some of the time.
There isn't always something right to say: Sometimes
words can't make things better, but silence, especially

combined with a loving touch, a hand on a hand, is a remarkable tool. It makes for powerful connections. You and your parent, side by side, can each think your own thoughts and know that you love each other.

How Often Should You Visit?

Visiting in hospitals can be draining, especially if a family member is in for a long stay. School and work and household chores go on regardless of what is happening in the course of the illness. So children of cancer patients frequently ask themselves: How often should I visit?

"It was dumb to go all the time," says Leanne. "You just kind of stood there—like, he would talk to you and in the middle of a sentence he would fall asleep—and you're like, okay, there goes that conversation. I used to bring my homework, but you can't really concentrate—there were two chairs, and my big sister and my mom got the chairs and I would wind up sitting on the floor." But Leanne's mother insisted that everyone in the family go to the hospital every evening at six and stay until ten, even though Leanne's dad had told her ahead of time that it wasn't necessary for them to be there every night. Leanne never complained to her mother about going, but she resented the long tedious hours and the problems it caused with the rest of her life.

Andrea, on the other hand, protested bitterly when her father was in the hospital, but her mother still dragged her along every night to visit him. Joseph's mother said she didn't see any point in Joseph's going and watching his father suffer. She told Joseph she didn't think it was good for him. But Joseph knew that his father was dying and wanted desperately to be with him in those last days, so he skipped school sometimes and sneaked into the hospital.

All three of these young people had different problems with visiting. Parents may wind up having the last word on how often a child visits, but it is important for each child to examine his own feelings and try to figure out what is right for him. And it is important for him then to express those feelings. A good rule of thumb suggested by one oncology nurse is to try to get to a place where you are not feeling overwhelmed—but also not staying home wondering what's going on—and not feeling guilty. When you feel good about the amount of time you spend visiting, you have probably found the proper balance. Obviously, based on that formula, the amount of visiting will be an individual decision and will vary from person to person and from situation to situation.

But what about hospital rules? The fact is that rules about visiting can be bent in many circumstances, so don't hesitate to express your needs to the hospital staff. One mother who felt better with all of her family around her managed to get a playpen put in her room so that the baby could come and visit, too. That way, she pointed out, no one had to stay home and baby-sit. She was polite but assertive in expressing her needs. You can be, too. If there aren't enough chairs for your parent's visitors, ask for more. If you want to come mornings during the summer so you can take an afternoon job, see if that can be arranged. The worst that can happen is that someone will tell you no.

Sometimes, as was mentioned earlier, transportation becomes a problem when children want to visit. If you don't drive, or don't have access to a car or public transportation, perhaps you can get another adult or an older friend to drive you. Most churches and temples are responsive to this kind of need and would probably be able to find a member of the congregation to help you. A teacher or counselor at school might have suggestions.

Finding your own means of transportation will help you work out a schedule that suits your own emotional state, your own needs. Try to be creative in finding someone to help with this problem.

When Your Parent Doesn't Want You to Visit

The amount of time you decide to spend visiting at the hospital may change as your parent's situation changes. A patient who is awake and alert is often more receptive to visits; one who is feeling terrible may prefer shorter visits or, for certain periods of time, no visits at all. Parents may also find excuses to have their children not come to the hospital because they don't want the children to see them in a certain condition. It is hard not to feel hurt when your parent says he doesn't want to see you, however good the reason may be, and there is not much anyone can say to ease that kind of hurt. But perhaps it will help you understand if you know that when a person is very seriously ill he sometimes needs to save his energy just to get through each day. A very ill person may honestly not have the energy to relate to someone, to express love even to those he loves most. But that doesn't mean that the love is not there; it just means that he can't communicate it right now. When your parent is feeling stronger he will most likely want company again. In most cases this turning away of loved ones is a temporary condition, perhaps a result of a bad reaction to a chemo treatment.

Suppose also that your sick parent allows your other parent in to see him but doesn't want to have the children visit. Often this is because the parent still feels he needs to protect his children; his turning them away (even though it may not be what you want) can be an expression of his caring, too.

When Your Parent Is in a Coma

New decisions about visiting sometimes need to be made if a sick parent goes into a coma. (Although a coma can be very frightening because it seems as if the patient has begun his final leave-taking, coma does not always mean death. Patients do come out of coma and get better.) Coma is not entirely understood, and no one can say precisely how much a person feels or hears when in this state. Should you keep on visiting a person who is in a coma? What do you do at the bedside?

Many medical people feel that it is important to comatose patients that they continue to receive stimulation and to know that they are loved and being cared for. No one can tell you exactly what to do: Again, you need to find that place that makes you feel comfortable with what you are doing. Peter sat with his father and read to him. Janice brought a tape recorder and played her dad his Dixieland tapes. Carly's family all sat together in the room and talked among themselves. Sandi came in every day and took her mother's hand, as the nurse suggested, and said, "I am Sandi, your daughter, and I want you to know I'm visiting you. I love you very much, and I'm here with you and holding your hand." And then Sandi would just sit as if her mother could hear (and maybe she could) and talk about her day.

Esteban visited the hospital every day at first when his father went into a coma, but as it continued he didn't stay as long; it made him feel too sad and helpless to see his father that way. Then, after a month and a half, Esteban started coming back to the hospital to sit in his father's room again. It was just something he wanted to do. He didn't know why.

Finding Your Own Way

You have to find your own way. As a teenager you have people telling you what to do half the time and expecting adult responsibility from you the other half. It isn't always easy to figure out what is the right way for you. Chances are you won't even be sure which role you like best from day to day. On the one hand, you might want to bow out of the whole complicated illness scene, or, on the other, you might feel excluded and want to get closer to your parent.

Most teenage children of cancer patients feel slighted when doctors or nurses come into their parent's room and automatically ask the child to leave. Most would feel better remaining and knowing what is being said, what is going on. If that is true of you, you may want to speak to your parents and let your needs be known. You can say, "I don't want this to upset you, but I would like to stay in the room when the doctor is there, to hear what he has to say, to ask some of the questions that have been bothering me."

You can also ask questions of the nurses or other people on the medical staff. If the person happens to be busy at the moment, ask when he or she will have time to talk to you. You have every right to do this. Most hospitals have chaplains (sometimes called Pastoral Care staff) and social workers who can help you also. You may have to take some initiative to find your niche in this hospital situation, to find some way to make yourself feel as comfortable as possible with what is going on, even to find support if your parents have nothing left at the moment to give you. You may need to find someone who can help you say to your parents: "Hey, this kid needs some space, needs to be out of this nightmare for a day or two. Give him a break." Many people in a hospital setting can help you with whatever you are going through. Keep asking until you find the right person.

If Your Parent Is Near Death

Sometimes, at the end of an illness, the hospital stay is a death vigil. It can be painfully difficult to leave the hospital at the end of the day not knowing if you will ever see your parent alive again. It is equally—if not more—difficult for the patient to say good night each night thinking that he might really be saying good-bye to everyone and everything he loves. Sometimes a patient finds it necessary to let go gradually before death actually comes, and it can hurt his family a great deal if they feel that he has lost the will to live when the family wants him to go on fighting. Many families also have to decide whether they will ask the doctors to use extreme measures to keep the patient alive as long as possible or to let him die naturally when it seems time for him to go.

Many of these issues surrounding the death of a parent are discussed in the chapters immediately following. The important thing to remember here is that you can't set up standards or expectations for yourself for this situation; you can't decide ahead of time how you will react; you mustn't judge yourself or let others judge you and say that you are handling the death the right way or the wrong way. You will handle it as you need to handle it.

Some children cry in the room of their sick parent; others do not. Some can express their love and their good-byes in words; others cannot. Mary knew that her mother was going to die soon. At first she had been afraid to go to the hospital, and she was really turned off by her mother's condition. But gradually she got used to the sights and sounds of the hospital floor, and she even got to the point where she was helping to feed her mother. Her mother, who had always been a very independent woman, cried when Mary first tried to do this, but Mary comforted her by saying, "You did so much for me all these years that I'm glad I can do this little bit for you." As her condition got worse, Mary's mother was moved to the ICU. Mary had to get up on a chair (with the hospital chaplain's help) to reach over all the tubes and machines and kiss her mother good-bye. It was hard to do, but it was something Mary felt was very important to her. The night Mary's mother died, Mary had gone to her best friend's high school graduation. She had hesitated about going, but the hospital chaplain and her father had asked her: "What do you think your mother would want you to do?" Mary knew her mother would have wanted her to go to the graduation. And she and her mother had already taken leave of each other the way they needed to. Mary had already told her mother good-bye.

Lewis was sitting by his father's bed and holding his hand at the moment he died. Karen and her family were in the waiting room with Karen's older sister who had just arrived from out of town. Karen and her father and brother had been at the hospital for three days around the clock, but none of them hapened to be in the room with Karen's mom when she died. The family went in together when they heard and cried together by her bedside.

Karl didn't want to go into his mother's room after she died; he was afraid that he would always see her dead in his mind, and he wanted to remember her alive. Louise got great comfort from the peaceful look on her father's face. Patrick couldn't stand the way his family were all sitting around his father's bed wailing. He went out and ran for miles on the streets around the hospital and then went home to hear the news. He knew nobody else would understand, but that was the way he had to do it.

If you think of dying as part of living, you will understand that even though this farewell to your parent is a unique and significant experience, all the other parts of your lives together are weighed in the balance, too. What you do, where you are at the moment of death is not necessarily the most important thing. Take time now, while your parent is alive, to say the things you want to say to him, to express your feelings as openly as you can. It doesn't matter whether you expect to have many more years together or just a few short weeks—it is important to try to have that time of sharing, difficult as it may be to get it started.

Being in the hospital makes people more aware of the fragility of life. It also puts people in a room together where they can talk, and perhaps it should be used as an opportunity to get important things said. But even for those of you who can't get those words out, be comforted by knowing that your parent has probably sensed your pain and your caring anyway. Lori couldn't tell her dad she loved him—she just couldn't get it said out loud. But when she left his hospital room two days before he died, her father did something Lori never forgot. He held up a hand and blew her a kiss and said, "Yeah, Lori. I love you, too."

Things to Do for a Parent in the Hospital

- Celebrate someone's birthday by having a party in your parent's room. Bring an extra wrapped present so that the patient has something to give to the guest of honor, too.
- Bring in family photos, preferably large ones, to put

in the hospital room. Photograph people, pets, and places.

- Make a large calendar on poster board and write on it what is happening or going to happen each day. (Days all merge together when a person is in the hospital for a long time.)
- Prepare for and celebrate holidays together— make holiday decorations.
- Make tape recordings of greetings from loved ones who can't visit regularly. Also share the outside world by taping a cat meowing, or birds singing, or a baby cooing.
- Send cards frequently so that the patient can look forward to mail-delivery time.
- Bring in an assortment of greeting cards (with stamps) for the patient to send to relatives and friends.
- Bring flowers from a garden, colored leaves, pine branches that smell like home.
- Stop by the room to let your parent see you all dressed up on the way to a party or prom.
- Bring someone new (a neighbor, one of your parent's friends, one of your own friends) to visit.
- Be sensitive to the patient's energy level. Offer to watch TV or listen to the radio with him if he seems tired. Sit without talking some of the time, just keeping him company.
- Sit down next to your parent instead of standing up and talking over him. It will be more comfortable for him to communicate with you that way.

CHAPTER 7

Why Did This Happen?

Why did this happen to you? Why was it your mom, or your dad, who had to get cancer? What has your family ever done to deserve such pain? Have you asked yourself such questions? It would be natural if you did, because people throughout the ages have done so when life seemed to give them a particularly unfair deal. People have always tried to make sense out of suffering. They have tried to find a way to live with seemingly unbearable unfairness. In the process, some of the questioners found answers that satisfied them. Many found them in religion, as will be discussed in the following pages. Others could find no adequate answers and had to seek instead a way to live with the questions. This also was often done in the context of religion.

When people need an explanation for suffering that can't otherwise be understood, one of the first sources they turn is to God. There are many different ways of looking at God's role in the apportioning of illness to people. Some say that the suffering of a person is the result of sin—not necessarily his sin, but sin going all the way back to Adam and Eve. Others, including clergypersons of many faiths, reject that idea entirely. No, they say, a person doesn't get cancer because God is displeased with him. God doesn't work that way. In fact, cancer is not part of God's plan. God's plan is for us to conquer diseases, to be as healthy as possible. It is health and happiness that God wants for God's people.

Some people have another explanation. We don't entirely understand it, they say, but "It's the will of God" that a person develops cancer. And God is not accountable to anyone for how He does things. Others, clergy included, reject that idea also. God is not masterminding individual lives, they say. Given a physical universe in which disease and suffering are present, every one of us is vulnerable to such things, and the fact that a particular tragedy strikes a particular person at a given time does not mean that God intended it as a lesson for that person.

Who Is Right?

Who is right? Why do some people have ready explanations and others none? One Catholic priest asks you to think about it this way. Many people are so uncomfortable, he says, at feeling helpless in the face of a loved one's distress that they come up with answers to make their own sense of helplessness go away. They might try to comfort a young person by telling him how beautiful it is in heaven and how happy his father will be to be with God. They tell him his father got cancer because his family was strong and God knew that they would be able to cope. They say that if his father dies, it will be because God needs his father more than he does.

But often the answers they give lead only to more anger or to alienation from God. "I need my dad more than God does right now," says one child of a cancer patient angrily. "My dad wanted to be in heaven more than he wanted to be with me," concludes another sadly. "It was our fault," decides another. "It was because our family is the way it is that God gave Dad cancer. It is because of us that God gave him this pain."

Rabbi Harold S. Kushner, whose son had a rare and terrible disease that killed him when he was only fourteen years old, thought long and hard about these questions of suffering and loss. He wrote down his thoughts in a book called *When Bad Things Happen to Good People*, which is highly recommended by clergypersons of all faiths to people of all faiths who suffer loss. It was Rabbi Kushner's conclusion that God doesn't cause bad things to happen to good people. In fact, he says, God doesn't cause our misfortunes at all.

> Some [of our misfortunes] are caused by bad luck, some are caused by bad people, and some are simply an inevitable consequence of our being human and being mortal, living in a world of inflexible natural laws. The painful things that happen to us are not punishments for our misbehavior, nor are they any way part of some grand design on God's part. Because the tragedy is not God's will, we need not feel hurt or betrayed by God when tragedy strikes. We can turn to Him for help in overcoming it, precisely because we can tell ourselves that God is as outraged by it as we are.[1]

---

[1] Kushner, Harold S., *When Bad Things Happen to Good People* (New York: Schocken Books, 1981), p. 134.

God, then, doesn't want the bad things to happen either, according to Kushner. Or, as an Episcopal clergyman puts it, God is not a sadistic God, which He would have to be if He intentionally caused cancer. Instead He is a caring God, a God Who is hurting with you and your family, a God Who hears you crying. This God wants to bring you comfort, not pain.

How Can Religion Help?

How can religion bring a grieving person comfort if God can't control the cancer? Many find comfort in praying. "My whole family would pray together," says nineteen-year-old Marcy. "We'd say Rosary together every night and go to church, and Mom would bring Communion home to Dad." Seventeen-year-old Patty tells how her uncle "set up this thing where we thought good things about my mom every day at three o'clock—we thought good things and prayed for her—and in some ways I think it helped her. I'd call her and she'd say, yeah, yeah, I felt better this afternoon. You get some hope from it, and I think you need hope, any way you can get it."

For those children of cancer patients who get comfort from their religious beliefs, that comfort can be powerful indeed. "It was prayer that got me through," said fifteen-year-old Connie. "I prayed all the time—sometimes it seemed like the only thing I *could* do. And it made me feel stronger."

Some Christian churches offer a healing service at which patients can ask for prayers for themselves or others can ask for prayers on their behalf. At healing services those who are sick can come forward for what is called "the laying on of hands." This anointment with oil, an ancient sign of soothing physical illness, is today a symbol of the power of healing given to the Church. It is accompanied by prayers, sometimes formal, sometimes extemporaneous. But not all the people prayed for get well. It can be very hard to pray for someone's recovery and then to feel that God has not answered your prayers. It can feel as if God has rejected you, as if your prayers weren't good enough. If God does have the power to change the course of your parent's illness, why doesn't He? And if He doesn't have that kind of power, what's the use of praying?

Many churches that incorporate a healing service into their program of worship make it very clear ahead of time that there is no guarantee that the cure prayed for will take place. But healing, they say, may still be granted. The healing they refer to, however, is not so much a cure (physical healing) as spiritual healing, a coming to terms with illness and death as part of the human condition. Many religions also offer faith in spiritual immortality or resurrection as a form of healing, because it lessens the fear of the possibility of death.

Other Purposes of Prayer

Prayers serve purposes other than asking a favor from God. "I was praying to the very end that Mom would get well," says Regina. "And even when she took a turn for the worse, I still thought she was going to get better. I couldn't imagine Mom not being around. And yet at the same time I *knew* she couldn't get better, not as bad off as she was at the end. I guess it was just a way of hoping." Regina was a nursing student: She knew better than most children of cancer patients the seriousness of her mother's condition, but she nevertheless was able to express her continuing hope through prayers. Prayers in this case were Regina's way of not giving in to despair.

PROPERTY OF
SOUTH KNOX SCHOOL CORP.

Prayers can also help you voice your anger and grief and pain. The psalms, says one scholar, "express the pain, grief, dismay, and anger that life is not good. (They also refuse to settle for things as they are, and so they assert hope)."[2] As one Episcopal minister puts it, God is not affronted when you express these strong and angry feelings through prayer—rather, He honors your anger, He honors your pain. He helps you by allowing you to express your feelings, and He comforts you by remaining with you.

Prayers often affirm that faith in God's continuing presence; they can be used almost as mantras are used in meditation, their repetition soothing, strengthening, reminding the believer that God has not deserted him. A famous story tells how Eddie Rickenbacker, a U.S. pilot during World War II, crashed with a crew of seven into the Pacific Ocean, where they floated on rafts for twenty-one days before being rescued. Reportedly, what kept that group of people going was a prayer session every day, and the prayer most often repeated was Psalm 139, part of which reads as follows:

Lord. . .
you are all around me, on every side;
you protect me with your power. . .
If I went up to heaven, you would be there;
if I lay down in the world of the dead,
you would be there.
If I flew away beyond the east,
or lived in the farthest place in the west,

---

[2] Brueggemann, Walter, *Praying the Psalms* (Winona, Minn.: Saint Mary's Press, Christian Brothers Publications, 1973), p. 28.

you would be there to lead me,
you would be there to help me...[3]

Your own favorite prayer may be able to help you as Psalm 139 helped Rickenbacker's crew on the Pacific Ocean. The pain of grief or impending loss can make you feel just as helpless and lost as that crew was. The feeling of God's continuing presence, however, can comfort you and make you feel less alone.

Life After Death

To many people, religion offers comfort in its assurance of a life after death. Most major religions have some concept of an afterlife, whether it be a place where life continues in some physical form, or a notion of spiritual immortality, or a feeling that the good a person does in this life has influence even after his death. To most Christians, life after death is primarily a reunion with God, but it is also thought of as a time when one will be together with loved ones who have died. The idea of this reunion with God and loved ones is so important to some people that they choose to think of death as a matter for "congratulation [rather] than condolence."[4] But most people realize that there is still a great deal of pain involved in the leave-taking, and they know that a grieving son or daughter does not want to be congratulated for the loss of a parent. Still, the idea that life

[3] Quoted in Link, Mark, S. J., *These Stones Will Shout* (Niles, Ill.: Argus Communications, 1975), p. 132.
[4] Harding, Rachel and Mary Dyson, *From the Private Letters of Industrious People: A Book of Condolences* (New York: Continuum Publishing Company, 1981), p. 62.

continues, that the loved one will be happy with God, that perhaps everyone will be together again in heaven, is a thought that can take away some of the immediate pain of loss.

Andreas says that when his father first found out how serious his cancer had become, he said to the family, "I'm ready to go, but if I don't go, that's fine, too. Either way I win." By winning either way, Andreas says, his father meant "that if he dies, he's going to see his dad again —his dad died when he was fifty—and my grandmother died recently, and he and my mom lost a few kids and he's planning on seeing them, too, on the way up." Andreas said it made everything easier on the family knowing that his dad wasn't too afraid of dying—"and I like knowing that whatever happens I'll see him again some day, too."

You do not have to believe in a life after death, however, to find comfort in religion. At a Jewish funeral, for example, eulogies are included in the service to recognize "not only that a death has occurred but that a life has been lived."[5] The gathering around of people who knew and loved a parent can be very comforting to a child who realizes, sometimes for the first time, how many people were touched by his parent's special gifts. If the parent was a teacher, for example, as Corey's father was, the child sees that his parent's legacy lives on in the lives of the students he taught or in the memories of people he worked with. In fact, Rabbi Kushner says, what religion does best is to put us in touch with other people as we share significant times of our life. In the sad times, "when we feel so terribly alone, singled out by the hand of fate, when we are

---

[5] Grollman, Rabbi Earl A., "The Jewish Way in Death and Mourning," in *Concerning Death: A Practical Guide for the Living*, ed. Earl A. Grollman (Boston: Beacon Press, 1974), p.126.

tempted to crawl off in a dark corner and feel sorry for ourselves, we need to be reminded that we are part of a community, that there are people around who care...and that we are still part of the stream of life."[6]

Finding Support in Your Congregation

Even people who are not particularly religious look to their place of worship for support in times of grief. Churches and temples are often prepared to provide transportation, to be "big brothers" or "big sisters" to young people who need a caring adult to talk to, to visit bedridden or housebound patients so that their families can have a break, to provide cooked meals and cheer and friendship. Many members of the clergy these days are trained as counselors and work with family members individually or as a group to help them work out some of the problems caused by serious illness.

In many old books and stories, the clergyman is called in only when a person is dying to administer last rites and to see the family through the moment of death. But these days families are encouraged to call on the clergyperson at any time during the illness for whatever support is needed. A clergyperson may talk to family members one-on-one or be moderator at a family council. (One Presbyterian minister recommends that all members of the family get together every six weeks or so to talk about how the illness is affecting everyone, to express feelings, and to try to work out solutions to problems.) A clergyperson may help the family work through their feelings about the use of life support systems (see below). He or she may deal with matters of day-to-day living (like finding someone to drive a

---

[6] Kushner, *When Bad Things Happen*, pp. 119–20.

patient to chemotherapy treatments) or matters of faith.

Serious illness in a family may affect different family members' religious beliefs in different ways. One member may have his faith strengthened by suffering, and another may lose faith entirely. A clergyperson can help family members see that each must do his own believing and must explore these matters in his own way.

The Issue of Life Support

If a cancer patient is thought to be no longer curable, a clergyperson may be called in along with the doctor and the patient's family to discuss how the patient wants the last stages of his illness to be handled. With modern medicine, machines can keep a dying (perhaps unconscious or suffering) patient alive for weeks and even months after that patient would have died if left alone. Many patients don't want to prolong their suffering and the suffering of their family any longer than necessary. But this is a very complicated and difficult decision to make. Some patients do want to fight death to the very end. Some want to die when their "natural" time comes, while their families want them to keep on fighting. The issue here is not hastening death—not, for example, helping a suffering loved one to commit suicide, which under present law in this country is illegal—but rather choosing whether or not to prolong life through artificial means.

Relatives of the patient may have different ideas on the subject, and medical advisers may disagree with family. From a religious point of view, however, both Christian and Jewish clergypersons agree that there is no religious reason to use artificial life support systems to prolong the dying process, although there is also no religious reason not to use the systems if the patient and the family want to do so. Members of the clergy agree also that it is the primary right of the *patient*, not of the family, to decide whether a particular treatment or surgery or machine is to be used. These matters, therefore, should be discussed with the patient, ideally early enough in the illness so that he or she is strong enough to consider them and to express wishes. Although it is a painful and difficult subject to bring up, most families of cancer patients find that when they do so, the patient is way ahead of them. He or she has already been thinking about life and death and usually welcomes an invitation to talk about how the various stages of his illness should be handled. But although the family enters into the discussion and loved ones are entitled to express their opinions, it is the patient who in the end has the right to have his or her own wishes met as much as possible.

If You Lose Faith

It was mentioned earlier that some people, when faced with extreme suffering and grief, lose their religious faith entirely. "You are not my Father as I was taught," they say bitterly to God. "All You are is a big failure. You say that You answer prayers; but You don't answer prayers. You say that You respond to cries for help; but I don't hear You responding. Why should I believe in You anyway?"

Suffering people lose faith in God, and sometimes they feel guilty about it. The feeling of guilt can be very painful and can keep them from making use of the counseling services of their clergyperson, and it also may cut them off from other support that their church or temple might be able to offer them. What they don't understand is that most ministers and rabbis are not surprised or offended at loss of faith under such circumstances. They do not cast a grieving person out because of questioning. They do not insist on belief that you do not have.

Many, many people go through this questioning process when their faith is tested by cancer or some other similar suffering. Some do lose their faith altogether. Some lose it for a time, and then find their way back to belief. In his book *A Gift of Hope*, Robert Veninga quotes a parent who was furious at God for the loss of a son. "I told God how angry I was. I questioned how He could have taken my son when I thought I had been a 'good' Christian. And you know, as I was venting my hostility toward God a strange thing happened. Somehow I just believed that God wouldn't get angry with me. *I believed that God knew who I was and why I was so angry and accepted me for who I am.* That belief—that I could be myself—was healing."[7]

Given time, just as feelings of faith change to doubt, feelings of doubt may be altered, too. Most clergypersons will tell you to be patient, to try to wait out the doubt. Veninga quotes a victim of multiple sclerosis as saying, "I always believed that God would take care of me. But when I was lifted into a wheelchair for the first time, I knew I had to find a faith that would sustain me in ways that my old one never could have done."[8] Your image of God may change. People perceive God differently according to their spiritual needs and capabilities at any given time. And religion can do different things for you at different times, too. Consider the following poem:

---

[7] Veninga, Robert, *A Gift of Hope: How We Survive Our Tragedies* (Boston: Little, Brown & Company, 1985), p. 213.
[8] Veninga, *Gift of Hope*, p. 221.

One day,
I decided to make God the center of my life.
This decision gave me unbelievable peace and joy.
But two days later,
I did something that no believer would ever do.
I was totally discouraged and concluded that I had not
  really committed myself to God at all.
I had only psyched myself into believing I had.
But then I realized something important.
I realized that when we commit ourselves to God,
we commit only that part of ourselves of which we are
  aware at the moment.
That's all any man can do.[9]

Religion, then, provides some people with answers. But if
you are questioning, it may also help you to frame or to
explore the questions. Living with cancer is in large
measure a matter of learning to live with questions. Many
people think that having answers is a mark of maturity, that
the older you get, the fewer questions you have to ask. But
most people come to learn that the mark of maturity
instead is knowing when to ask for help with the questions.
There are always questions when it comes to matters of life
and death and God. Nobody knows the answers for certain.
In fact, that is what faith is all about.

When Loss of Faith Leads to Thoughts of Suicide

When the pain of losing someone or watching a loved one
suffer combines with loss of faith, some people feel so dev-

---

[9] Link, *These Stones Will Shout*, pp. 56–57.

astated that they contemplate suicide. If you feel this way, seek help immediately. (See pp. 64–66 for more information on suicidal feelings.) Here, too, religion (even without active faith) can help you through. Keep in mind that your clergyperson has seen many other people through similar crises. "Bring your suffering to speech," as one Catholic priest advises. Ask your questions—ask any that you want, and express your anger and your doubt through your questions. Getting anger out is a good and healthy way to combat depression. You have a right to be angry. Life has dealt you a frightening blow, and the old answers may seem very inadequate in the face of your new questions.

Most religions do counsel against suicide, and all the clergypersons consulted for this book agreed that in no case was suicide a good or appropriate solution for teenagers. Consider, they said, that life is a gift of God, a gift not to be taken lightly, even if it doesn't seem worth much right now. Consider that death is not what your parent would have wanted for you. Consider that once you are dead there is no turning back. When you are alive, you can make things better. Once you are dead, you lose that chance.

If your religious beliefs counsel against suicide, listen to them. Julie did, and as a result she got a second chance she might not otherwise have had. She lost faith in many ways while her mother was near death, but that teaching against suicide remained with her. "The only thing I think religion did help me with," she says, "was not killing myself. Because there were so many times I had that powerless feeling that I looked for reasons and ways—you know, I looked for pills in the house—I even took some once because I was so depressed but all they did was put me to sleep for an hour or so because I didn't take very many. I didn't want to do it, but I wanted someone to know how unhappy I was. I was saying, Come on, listen to what I'm doing—but I wouldn't really do it because religion to me is, like, if you kill yourself, that's a mortal sin."

Julie can see now that her despair, although infinitely painful at the time, was only one phase of her cycle of grief. She is glad now that she is alive. Keep your eye on life, Rabbi Kushner counsels. "We need to get over the questions that focus on the past and on the pain—'Why did this happen to me?'—and ask instead the question which opens doors to the future: 'Now that this has happened, what shall I do about it?'"[10] William McCullough, a Presbyterian minister, agrees. "To pick up and move on at the right time," he says, "is an essential part of the truly religious life."[11]

Don't deny the questions, or the grief that produced them. "The answers may never be totally found," says Veninga, "*but by becoming a friend to the questions* a small step towards inner healing is taken."[12] Allow yourself faith, if you have it, but also allow yourself doubt. And most of all, allow yourself *time*.

"I feel very, very sorry for whoever doesn't have God on their side," says fifteen-year-old Charity, whose father died of throat cancer after a long illness, "because when death happens if you don't have God, you won't have nobody, not anything at all." "After my mother died," says seventeen-year-old Dave, "everyone was telling me she'd gone to heaven and was happy with God. I didn't want to hear it. I still don't want to hear it. My mom and I used to go to

---

[10] Kushner, *When Bad Things Happen*, p. 137.
[11] McCullough, William, "From Two Vantages: A Physician-Minister's Views," *But Not to Lose: A Book of Comfort for Those Bereaved*, ed. Austin H. Kutscher (New York: Frederick Fell, Inc., 1969), p. 32.
[12] Veninga, *Gift of Hope*, p. 211.

church all the time, but I haven't been to church since she died. What do I want to hear that church stuff for?"

When people are suffering, what works for one person doesn't necessarily work for another. Charity's faith sustained her, but the words of fellow church members only made Dave feel angry and alienated. People will offer you many words of comfort in the days that follow as well as a variety of explanations for what you are going through. But you are entitled in the end to find your own explanations and your own comfort. The answers to your questions may not be easy to come by, and sometimes it will seem that there are no answers at all. But it may help if you know that questions can also be a life force. Ask your questions, and see where they lead you.

What Happens When Someone Dies?

Throughout the ages, all over the world, death has been considered a mystery. People have looked to myth and philosophy and religion as well as to science for explanations of the phenomenon of death, for clues to what might happen to a person after his life on earth has ended. Does life in some other form continue? Does everything end when a person dies? Until modern times, death used to come most often at home, not in a hospital, and young people were not shielded from the subject of death and the act of dying as they are today. People were afraid of death as an unknown and saddened by it, but they were also more familiar with it and more inclined to accept it ultimately as part of the life cycle. And they were not as afraid of their dying loved ones as people sometimes are today.

"We were called to the hospital because they said she wouldn't make it through the night," says Anna, "and I was going the whole way saying, do it now before we get there.

Let's get it all over with so we don't—so *I* don't have to be there. I mean, I knew my dad wanted us to be there in time, but I was thinking of myself, and at that time I didn't want to go through that. I kept saying, just now, please. Do it now."

Anna reports being terrified about her dying mother because she had no idea what the experience would be like. Anna had never seen someone die; she hadn't even been permitted to go to her grandparents' funerals. In addition, she hadn't seen her mother in several weeks, because the adults in the family had decided her mother was too sick to have the children visit, so Anna felt distant from her mother already. Did her mother know that she was dying? Was she scared? What would she, Anna, say to her? What were you supposed to *do* when someone was dying? Would there be a doctor there? What if Anna were alone in the room at the time her mother died? What if she got hysterical? What if someone made her kiss her mother after her mother was already dead?

As discussed in Chapter 6 on hospital visits, it would have been easier for Anna if she had asked ahead of time what she would encounter when she saw her mother. "Your mother has lost a lot of weight," her father might have told her. "Her skin is yellow because of liver problems, and she looks very different from when you last saw her, so don't be shocked. She's hooked up to a lot of machines, and sometimes she moans and thrashes around like she is in a lot of pain. But the doctors say she is getting too many painkillers to be feeling much pain now. She probably won't know consciously that we are there, but maybe on some level she will, and that will be comforting to her. Just stand by her bed when we get there and tell her you love her. Whether or not she hears you, you'll know you've said it. We'll just stay in the room after that and keep her company, but you can leave if it gets to be too much for you. It will be hard, but it won't be impossible. And then at some point Mom's body will probably relax and we'll know she's gone. We've made a decision not to put her on a respirator, because she has no hope of living at this point and she doesn't want to prolong her dying. There'll be nurses and doctors around, and we can call them if she needs anything."

The above is only one scenario, because each death is different, just as each life and each illness is different. Some people die peacefully, seeming just to slip away; others, unfortunately, seem to die struggling with pain or fear. But each particular death proceeds from the person's own medical history, colored by the surroundings in which he dies, by his personality and that of his family. The point is that if you have been close to your parent's illness all along, the actual moments of death may not seem as alien and frightening as you would think. Your parent's dying will be the last act of his living.

Definitions of Death

What is death? What does science say about it? It is, first of all, a natural part of the life cycle, the return to earth of the physical remains of those who die so that those remains can nourish other living things. But how do we know when a person is dead? Finding an answer to that question is not as simple as it may seem.

It used to be that a person was considered dead when his heart stopped beating and he stopped breathing, because loss of those functions would necessarily cause his brain to die. But with the development of modern medical techniques and mechanical devices that can keep blood and oxygen circulating, new definitions of death were needed.

Most authorities now use brain-oriented criteria to determine and define death. Opinions differ on this still, but it is generally accepted that (with certain specific exceptions) a person is dead if for twenty-four hours he is "unconscious, does not move, either voluntarily or involuntarily, does not respond to anything, shows no brain activity on an electroencephalogram machine, and cannot breathe without mechanical aid. . . . [1] Certain of the person's organs may remain alive, however, maintained on machines after brain activity has stopped, and physicians can sometimes remove those organs and use them in transplants. You can see how the technology of organ transplants necessitated a rethinking of the beating-heart definition of death, because otherwise the removal of a heart for transplant, for example, might be considered the act that killed the patient.

In fact, in a court case in California, a man named Andrew Lyons was charged with shooting another man named Samuel Allen in the head. Allen was later pronounced dead, but because only his brain had been damaged doctors kept his body alive with artificial life support systems so his heart could be used in a transplant operation. Lyons, defending himself against a homicide charge, brought a lawsuit that accused the doctors of causing Allen's death by removing his heart; Lyons maintained that death had been caused by that act, not by the bullet to the brain. The case was decided based on the judge's definition of death in his instructions to the jury. Judge William J. Hayes told the jury that "a person may be pronounced dead if, based on usual and customary standards of medical practice, it is determined that the person

[1] Klein, Stanley, *The Final Mystery* (Garden City, N.Y.: Doubleday & Company, Inc., 1974), p. 12.

has suffered an irreversible cessation of brain function."
Lyons was found guilty of manslaughter.[2]

These are very complicated issues, with implications far
beyond any individual case. People differ even about the
generally accepted definition of brain death. Who should
decide which definition of death to use? How can you be
sure that damage to the brain in a particular case is irreversible? To what extent can the patient and his family decide
for themselves which life-maintaining treatments and
devices should be used and when to stop them? What is
the role of living wills, which instruct doctors not to continue treatment the only purpose of which is to delay the
inevitable death of the signer? What if doctors and nurses
feel they can't go along with a patient's wishes because of
their own legal or moral obligations?

Moral and Religious Perspectives

The scientific definitions of death often merge with feelings
based on moral or religious beliefs. Many people, as discussed in Chapter 7, feel that matters of life and death
are not fully explainable by science or logic. Although no
one can see or define the human spirit or soul, people all
over the world and throughout the ages have believed that
within each person there is a spirit that can exist apart from
the body. This spirit or soul is considered to represent the
essence of that particular human being. In some belief
systems the spirit is thought to go to a spirit world after
death, sometimes with the ability to return occasionally to
the land of the living. In many belief systems the spirit is

---

[2] Quoted in Humphry, Derek and Ann Wickett, *The Right to Die* (New
York: Harper & Row, 1986), p. 284.

punished or rewarded in death for acts during life. The traditional Christian belief, for example, is in a heaven in which the souls of believers who have led worthy lives will live eternally in peace and happiness. The story of Jesus's life and death and resurrection is thought to show that although all people must die, death can be overcome with faith. On the other side of death, most Christians believe, is reunion with God and loved ones and eternal life.

There are many variations of this attempt to understand the soul, the personality, the nonphysical characteristics of a person that seem to represent the essence of a life. Some people think the individual soul is a tiny part of God or of a Universal Soul that returns to its origin when the body dies. The traditional Buddhist view is that the soul is born again and again in different bodies until it can free itself from worldly desires and attachments. Whatever the specifics of the belief, the core of it is that the soul separates from the body when the body dies. The body dies, and the spirit lives on.

A person is not dead then, according to this way of thinking, until the spirit separates from the body. Most people probably agree with this intuitively, although they could not say at what moment that separation takes place or how exactly it fits together with the condition of brain death that is the scientific determinant of death. What is significant, however, is the conclusion (which is going to sound obvious) that a person therefore is alive as long as he is alive. What is meant by this is that being dead is different from *dying*. Dying is a process of living. When people are dying, they don't become different people, although they may have new and different concerns and problems. It is natural to be afraid of death, perhaps, but it becomes easier to deal with a dying person if you remember that he or she is just a person going through an inevitable phase of living.

How Do You Behave with a Dying Person?

"When we found out about Mom," says Eileen, "the scariest thing of all was how was I going to face her. I didn't know what I was going to say or what I was going to do. I talked to her on the phone at the hospital and told her how I felt, and you know—she helped me through it. She had seen four or five of her friends die, and she knew how she felt, so she could tell me."

"I was afraid," said Tomas. "I thought something was going to be different now that it was out in the open that Dad was probably going to die. I thought, Would he not talk to me because of something, or if I said something wrong would he be mad at me? Would he ignore me? But nothing like that happened."

"You are one with one who is dying the same way you are with yourself," says Stephen Levine in a book on the subject of dying. "Open, honest, and caring. You are simply there, listening with a heart that is willing to hold the joy or pain of another with equal capacity and compassion. If it hurts, it hurts. If it makes you happy, it makes you happy. Not trying to change things. Not trying to make something or someone other than it is. Just hear the truth that the moment has to offer."[3]

"Dying," says Levine in another part of his book, "doesn't have to be hell. It can be a remarkable opportunity for spiritual awakening. I have been with many people who have experienced this falling away of energy, this... wearing away of the body, this inability to be the individual they thought they were, who, instead of tightening into

---

[3] Levine, Stephen, *Who Dies: An Investigation of Conscious Living and Conscious Dying* (Garden City, N.Y.: Anchor Press/Doubleday, 1982), pp. 157–158.

even greater suffering, began to let go of the root of their contraction. . . . Such people notice that even though the energy decreases, though they may never leave their bed or work again, . . . even though they are watching their body deteriorate, somehow their spirit and their participation in the moment are getting stronger and stronger."[4]

Have you ever before thought of dying in those ways? Have you heard the words "opportunity" or even "adventure" used in connection with the act of dying? Has your mom or dad? At some point, can you share these points of view with your parent? If your parent should ultimately be dying of cancer, can you help your family go through the process of dying as a family—everyone included? What is the state of your parent's illness right now? How is he or she feeling about it? Do you know? Can you ask? Because you may be surprised to find out how different people react when facing their own death. Novelist May Sarton describes in the following way the reaction of a fictional character who has just come to terms with the news that she is going to die of lung cancer:

> What had become almost uncontrollable grief at the door now seemed a blessed state. It was not a state she could easily define in words. But it felt like some extraordinary dance, the dance of life itself, of atoms and molecules, that had never been as beautiful or as poignant as at this instant, a dance that must be danced more carefully and with greater fervor to the very end.[5]

---

[4] Levine, *Who Dies*, p. 57.
[5] Sarton, May, *A Reckoning* (New York: W.W. Norton & Company, Inc., 1978), p. 9.

Stephen Levine quotes a thirty-one-year-old woman with a brain tumor:

> You don't have a moment to lose to tell people how much you love them. In a way I am freer to express my love now than I ever was before. All my life I wanted to tell people how much I loved them but I felt I couldn't...I feared they wouldn't listen. It seemed like the time was just never right. But now I see I don't have a moment to lose.[6]

Saying "I love you" seems to be a big part of the experience of dying. So does valuing and appreciating the remaining days and hours and relationships of life. Being together with loved ones is also important.

"If we were just watching TV I made sure I did it with Dad," says Danielle. "I studied in the room with Dad there —and we had some fun time, some jokes time. Spending all the time I did with him was just wonderful while I had him, because I knew I was going to lose him. A friend of mine whose father died of a heart attack told me she was jealous of that fact—because I could tell my dad I loved him and kind of say good-bye to him in my own way. She was really jealous of that."

There are good and meaningful moments, then, in being with a dying person, but there can also be great anguish. Since it is the premise of this book that cancer patients and their families are best served by honesty, you need to be told here that saying good-bye to a parent, especially one who may be suffering greatly in the last stages of cancer, can be a very painful experience as well as a rewarding or

---

[6] Levine, *Who Dies*, pp. 75–76.

fulfilling one. Not all cancer patients suffer greatly, but some do, and pain combined with loss of various body functions can be a tremendously difficult thing to see and to endure. Often loved ones are in awful conflict, wanting to keep the sick person with them as long as possible, but also needing to see the suffering end. The following two quotations describe that terrible conflict in different ways. The first is a quotation from a book by Betty Rollin, whose mother had been battling cancer for a long time. The moment Ms. Rollin describes is the moment right after a telephone conversation with her mother's doctor when she is told that her mother has only several more months to live:

> When we hung up I did something I hadn't done for a long while. I sat down on the edge of my bed, and I covered my face with my hands and cried. It was a good cry, and it felt terrible and wonderful the way good cries do. To this day I'm not sure whether I was crying because my mother was going to live or because she was going to die. Part of me wanted her to die, so "several months" sounded like a long time, given what she was going through and that it could only get worse. And part of me couldn't bear for her to die, and to that part "several months" sounded like tomorrow. I hated both choices and what I hated most of all was knowing they were not choices.[7]

The second quotation, a poem to a dying parent by Linda Pastan, expresses a longing that the parent can free himself from life and therefore from his suffering. Deep

---

[7] Rollin, Betty, *Last Wish* (New York: Linden Press/Simon & Schuster, 1985), p. 142.

love and compassion for the dying parent are the motiva-
tion for the poet's wish. Ms. Pastan writes:

You have grown wings of pain
and flap around the bed like a wounded gull
calling for water, calling for tea, for grapes
whose skin you cannot penetrate.
Remember when you taught me
how to swim? Let go, you said,
the lake will hold you up.
I long to say, Father let go
and death will hold you up....[8]

Feelings run deep when a family member is dying.
Seemingly totally contradictory feelings can exist side by
side in a single person. You can, as Betty Rollin wrote,
wish for death and for life at the same time. You can love
and be angry, love and hate, be distraught and/or relieved
and/or guilty. Any combination of any feelings is possible,
and different family members can react to a given situation
in totally different ways. If the loved one's death is a slow
one, exhaustion makes all the problems worse. It is because
this process of living with dying can be so hard for both the
patient and his family that help is sometimes needed. One
organization that helps families with terminally ill patients
is Hospice.

The Hospice Way

Hospice provides care to terminally ill patients and their
families on the theory that such patients should be helped
to live life fully, in their own home surroundings if pos-

---

[8] Quoted in Viorst, Judith, *Necessary Losses* (New York: Simon &
Schuster, 1986), p. 263.

sible, until death comes of its own accord. It is the Hospice philosophy that a person with a terminal illness should be thought of not as a dying person but a living person, with a right to participate in decisions concerning his own care, to express his feelings, to be treated with dignity, to have help from and for his family in accepting his death.

"Hospices," says Anne Munley in *The Hospice Alternative*, "do not view death as a failure. They acknowledge that death is natural to human existence, and offer the dying safe passage in their journey from life to death—a passage in which dignity and important relationships are preserved, patients and families have a voice in planning care, and death is as pain-free and as meaningful as possible."[9]

Hospice doesn't attempt to cure, since it works only with patients whose illness is no longer curable. It tries instead to help its patients focus on goals that are still possible, such as good physical pain control, ability to remain at home rather than go into the hospital, freedom from spiritual and psychic distress, and good and open communication with loved ones.

Hospice works with the patient's own doctors. It works in somewhat different ways in different areas, but the emphasis is on providing support and training to the patient and the family to keep the patient at home as long as possible. At home the patient has more control over what is happening to him; he doesn't have to eat on a hospital schedule or limit his visitors to certain hours or take medication if he chooses not to do so. Hospice has registered nurses who go to a patient's home and teach family members to do many skilled nursing tasks. Family may, for example, give the patient medicine or manage diet or

---

[9] Munley, Anne, *The Hospice Alternative* (New York: Basic Books, Inc., 1983), pp. 35–36.

change catheter bags. Hospice nurses visit the home regularly and are generally responsible for coordinating care. Family can get help also from Hospice home health aides and social workers, from clergy associated with the program, and from trained Hospice volunteers who willingly pitch in to help with care when family members need a break from responsibility.

In addition, Hospices usually have a twenty-four-hour hotline so that family members can reach a trained nurse whenever they have urgent questions. "When it got down to the end," Sherry says, "Mom was on the phone with the Hospice nurse—I think every hour she kept calling her. Dad's blood pressure dropped real low and Mom about lost it, and that's when she started calling, because the doctors weren't real fast about calling back—I mean, they weren't bad, but it wasn't soon enough for Mom because she wanted to do something for him right then and she had no idea what to do—so the Hospice nurses really came in handy." Hospice nurses usually come to the home even at night if there is an emergency that the family can't handle with phone advice alone.

Caring for the Patient at Home

Hospice, in short, helps the family to care for the terminally ill patient in his own home. The psychological benefit to the patient can be enormous, and this in turn comforts family members who can be doing something positive to help their loved one. Children, by caring for a sick parent, can actively give back some of what that parent has given to them. And that feels good.

"It seems little," says Robby, "but I know what meant most to Dad about staying home was when we figured out how to get his hospital bed into the living room. He had put the bay window in just before he got sick, and this way he got the chance to look through it."

"It wasn't as hard as you would think," says Sherry. "Everyone says that must have been something—to have this bed in your dining room and not have any space to yourself and him always being there—and you were always cooking for him and making special stuff for him—but you look back and think, I'm glad we got to have him there. I'm glad we were the ones who were doing those things for him, and not someone he didn't even know."

Support for the Family

In addition to the family's *giving* care, the family also *gets* care from Hospice—support in their job of providing for their terminally ill patient. If things get too bad—if the patient has excessive pain, or develops an infection, or has breathing problems that can't be managed at home—the patient can be taken to a Hospice facility for care. Most Hospices have beds in local hospitals and some have their own separate facility where patients can be cared for until they are stable enough to return home.

Sometimes families keep a patient at home until death is imminent but then choose to take him or her to the Hospice unit to die. Hospice units are set up to be welcoming and homelike. Family members of all ages (even small children) may visit, pets are allowed, special foods to tempt a patient can be prepared, and the staff and volunteers are open and warm and supportive and very much attuned to the special needs of a terminally ill patient and his family. And Hospice helps the family even after the patient dies. All Hospices have bereavement programs, which offer professional and volunteer counseling and support to grieving families after the death of their loved one.

What Kind of Families Use Hospice?

Hospice is not appropriate for everyone. It is not right for the family determined at all costs to delay the death of the patient with every medical and mechanical means. It is not for patients who are able to get around on their own or still have a chance for a cure or a good remission. In some Hospice programs the patient must be homebound. It is not for families whose situation makes it impossible for them to care for a seriously ill patient at home over a long period of time. Sometimes a family is interested in Hospice but the patient wants no part of it.

To qualify for Hospice at all, (1) a patient must be diagnosed with a terminal illness, a progressive disease that gives him a life expectancy of six months or less; (2) he and his family must understand the Hospice program and the extent to which the family participates in the care of the patient; and (3) both the patient and his family must understand fully that the Hospice program is not designed to treat for cure (because cure has already been medically determined not to be possible) but rather to manage pain and to try to make the patient physically and psychologically comfortable for the remaining days of his life. Pain can't always be eliminated entirely, but it can usually be controlled by Hospice methods to a tolerable level.

Hospice is not, as is sometimes thought, a program that helps people to die. What it seeks to do instead is to help people stay alert and to live to the fullest *until they die*. Hospice and family and patient all work together to accomplish that goal. Usually they all learn and grow and gain comfort and satisfaction in the process.

Your parents may not be aware that Hospice is Medicare/Medicaid-certified and normally covered under traditional third-party payers (private insurance).

Other Alternatives

The rather long discussion of Hospice is not meant to imply that Hospice is the only good solution for terminally ill cancer patients. But it is a solution that is becoming increasingly popular. Most cancer patients who die today, however, still do so in traditional hospitals. In hospitals, treatment of terminally ill patients is often more aggressive, in the sense that the emphasis is on keeping the patient alive as long as possible. In a modern hospital setting, death may be seen essentially as a failure—a failure of science to keep the person alive[10]—whereas the Hospice philosophy is that once death is inevitable it should be accepted as a natural end to the process of living. Hospitals can still be sensitive and flexible in the care of their patients, however, and doctors in traditional hospital settings also take their patients' individual needs and wishes into account when planning treatment. Patients and families should explore alternatives and discuss these matters openly and make their wishes known to their doctors. You have a right to input on how these very important matters should be handled.

Funerals, Wakes, Memorial Services

Dying, then, is a part of life. But with death, life is ended. Whether the death takes place at home or in the hospital, a doctor is called in to certify the death, and then the body is usually removed to a funeral home or a crematorium, depending on the wishes of the family. In some cases an

---

[10] Stephenson, John A., *Death, Grief and Mourning: Individual and Social Realities* (New York: The Free Press, 1985), p. 34.

autopsy may be performed in the hospital, or the body may be donated for research.

Laws set out what must be done when a person dies, whatever the cause of death. These laws are basically for the purpose of protecting the health of the living by making sure that the physical remains are properly disposed of, and for collecting and recording vital statistics. In addition, customs such as funerals and wakes have grown up around death for the further purpose of supporting the people remaining and helping them to deal with their grief and fear in the face of death. Funeral ceremonies often try to explain, to make sense out of death. They bring home the reality of death. At a time when people feel alone and help-less, funerals provide social contact and give mourners something to do.

Viewing the Dead Body

Sometimes the body of the person who has died is on dis-play at the funeral or the wake. The body is embalmed at the funeral home (a fluid is injected into the arteries to replace the blood) to clean and disinfect the corpse and to slow down the process of decomposition. Cosmetics are usually used to make the body look at rest and peaceful. Relatives and other loved ones have differing reactions to this process. Some are comforted because the peaceful face of the dead person makes them feel that his suffering after the long illness is now truly over. Others feel that the makeup looks artificial and wrong. "Why couldn't they leave him alone?" they ask. "That doesn't look like Dad (or Mom)!" Some people think that putting makeup on the corpse and making it look almost "alive" denies the reality of death and makes it harder for loved ones to accept the death. "I was there," says Lena, "and I can remember seeing her and I was looking at her and waiting for her to breathe—I mean, you're just waiting for her, just waiting for her, and it's weird—she looks okay, and you're just waiting for her to sit up...." At a time when it is very hard to make the transition from thinking of someone as alive to accepting the fact that he or she is dead, this kind of treatment of the dead body may make that process even more difficult.

Most experts on the grieving process now seem to think that it is good for the mourner to be able to see and perhaps touch the dead body of a loved one at some point in the funeral process as a way of truly confronting the reality of his death. They feel that experiencing death in this way is important later on in the mourning process. Not everyone agrees, and the needs and wishes of the family of the dead person certainly have to be taken into consideration. You may feel, for example, that touching or kissing a dead body is something that you would never want or be able to do. It may make you feel horrible even to think of it. You may feel that you would always want to remember your parent alive, not dead. You may feel one thing now but change your mind when the need arises to make that decision again at the time of your parent's death.

The sight of a dead loved one is painful, says Harriet Schiff in *The Bereaved Parent*, a book that has many wise things to say about loss and mourning, "much as cauterizing a wound is painful. Just as healing may not begin without that very painful procedure, psychiatrists believe that the same principle applies to viewing the body."[11] Viewing the body, Ms. Schiff feels, is important for aiding the long-term process of grieving. Many people are also

_____

[11] Schiff, Harriet Sarnoff, *The Bereaved Parent* (New York: Penguin Books, 1977), p. 14.

greatly comforted in later years by the good-byes they say to a dead loved one, by a last touch or a final farewell gesture. It is hard to view that body now, but will it help you later? That is a decision you have to make.

Some people choose one way, some choose another. Some people say good-bye in the hospital, some in the funeral parlor, some at the burial ceremony. Some say their good-byes alone with the dead body; others prefer to have someone with them to make them feel stronger. Some people say good-bye from a distance; others wish to touch and maybe kiss the dead person. And some people, in the end, choose not to see the body at all. They may already have said their good-byes while the person was alive, or they will say them at some time in the future, perhaps in a private moment of remembering, or at church on a Sunday morning, or months later at the cemetery. It is important to remember when you are making this decision that the decision is for *you*, not for your dead mom or dad (who can no longer be affected by the decision) or for your relatives or family friends (who must make their own decisions as to what is best for *them*). You may not in the end make the perfect decision—there will always be "what ifs" either way you decide. But if the decision you make is the best one for you at the moment, that is all anyone can ask of you and all you can ask of yourself.

What Are Funerals Like?

Have you ever been to a funeral? Many teenagers haven't because, as mentioned earlier, adults often still think of death as something from which they must shield their children. Many young people, when they do go, find themselves impatient with the whole idea of funerals. They find them artificial, phony, a waste of money, intensely uncomfortable. They would rather be alone with their family instead of having their grief made so public. They are uneasy when other people break down and cry around them. They feel very much exposed. They get furious when after the ceremony everyone gathers to eat and drink on an occasion that is supposed to be solemn and sad.

It may help to recall the purpose behind the funeral and other ceremonies surrounding a death. As mentioned earlier, it is necessary for the public health that the body be disposed of—either cremated or buried. It is thought useful for grieving people to be surrounded and supported at that time by others who love them and who loved and respected the person who died. Many funerals are religious ceremonies, and religion offers comfort to many grieving people, too. Religion can also aid psychologically in the task of mourning. In fact, there is an ancient wisdom in some of these traditions that sounds a lot like what psychiatrists and psychologists teach us today about dealing with loss.

In the Jewish religion, for example, there was a traditional formula for mourning the dead. Before the funeral, visitors were asked to stay away from the home so that the family had time for private weeping. The reason for this was probably an understanding that grief was "the natural expression of a significant relationship which. . . [had] just been terminated; [that] to comfort the mourners prematurely. . . [was] to insult the significance of the relationship."[12] The funeral itself, however, was public so that the community could share the loss and support the family in its grief. A casket containing the body was present so that the mourners couldn't deny the fact of the death.

---

[12]Kutscher, *But Not to Lose*, p. 67.

After the burial, food was to be eaten as a symbolic first step in bringing the mourners to accept the fact that life was to go on even though they were grieving.

The traditional grieving process, too, was carefully scheduled. The first seven days following the death were a time of intense and concentrated grieving in the home. After this the mourner was to go to temple and say prayers twice a day, thus being forced out of his house and into the company of other people, including other mourners, so that he might feel less singled out and alone. This twice-daily recitation of prayers for the dead was to last for eleven months, at which time a grave marker was to be set up over the dead person's grave and the formal mourning period was to end. The Kaddish, or prayer for the dead, was still said at certain times of the year, however—such as on the anniversary of the loved one's death—because sadness for a loss and the need to honor and remember a dearly loved person is never finished entirely. The whole process, if you think about it, encouraged healthful grieving and also guided the person gradually back into a more normal existence.

Although many funerals have religious content, some people are not religious and choose to give the death of a loved one significance in other ways. A family may have a nonreligious memorial service where people get together and remember the person who died; a number of the person's friends and admirers make speeches and share memories. There may be music at both religious and non-religious memorial ceremonies. If the body of the dead person is to be cremated, or if it is to be donated for medical research, there may be no burial service but instead some kind of ceremony to permit friends to offer their support to the family and pay their respects to the person who has died. People send flowers or make contributions to charities as a way of showing the family that they cared about the dead person.

How to Behave at a Funeral

How are you supposed to behave at a funeral? There is no right or wrong way. No one knows ahead of time exactly how he will react to intense grief. Everyone expected Leon to cry, but he found he wasn't ready to cry. When the minister came up to comfort him, he just said, "Fine. I know she's going to heaven. I don't want to talk about it anymore." His father told him he was being rude, but Leon wasn't being rude. He was just coping the only way he knew how to cope right then, by keeping his feelings inside, by relating to other people as little as possible.

Jeanine, on the other hand, couldn't sit still at her mother's wake. "They all told me to sit down," she remembers, "but I could *not* sit down. I just walked around and talked to everyone, and they were all telling me these stories, and I held my composure pretty well until I went downstairs with my best friend. And we were sitting there talking and it finally hit me what was going on. I mean—okay, it was all over now, here goes the end of coming home and finding her there, here goes the end of telling her when I make the softball team, when I did this or that—because I always did, I always thought of telling her first thing. And I couldn't go back upstairs after that, even though they kept telling me to. I just couldn't face those people again."

Neil remembers his mother's funeral: "At her funeral I was okay, and as soon as I got home I ate something and went out and played. Everybody was, like—hey, he doesn't care anything about his mother, he's out there playing and he isn't even crying or nothing. But now, when I feel like this and I can't stop feeling like this, they think this is the time I should be getting over it."

Jo remembers: "At the funeral I was fine—I was seriously fine—and I came home and everything, but then I got up and walked out of the room where everybody was and I just broke down—I mean, all over the place—I started throwing things all over the room, I started yelling, and afterward everybody said they didn't know what to do with me."

Everybody reacts differently. Some people want to talk about their loved one, others don't want to talk. Some people cry noisily, others act as if nothing big has happened. Some people tell jokes, others say nice things about the person who has died, still others are locked in anger at that person's having left them. There is no one right way. There is also no one right way for a family to handle the death of a loved one. People may criticize the way your family handles funeral arrangements (especially if you don't have a traditional funeral), but you are entitled as a family to do it your way. There can be laughter as well as tears, negative characteristics remembered as well as positive ones, a public ceremony or a private one.

The funeral, the memorial service, the wake are all intended to be rites of passage, acknowledgments of the end of a life. They will not, of course, be the end of grieving for your parent, nor the end of remembering. For a time right after the death you may even feel your parent's presence in a very active way.

"When Mom first died," remembers seventeen-year-old Earl, "I would still see her in the window each day when I was coming home from school. I used to run to her."

Lakeisha had a similar, very vivid experience. "This is going to sound strange," she recalls, "but the day after Dad died—we have this garage he built and there's a refrigerator in it and everything—and someone sent me out to get a pop or something for one of our guests and I heard this voice calling, 'Lakeisha.' And I said, 'Yeah?' And I heard this voice say, 'Lakeisha, I love you,' and then it just faded away in the wind. And I think maybe it was my father telling me everything was going to be all right."

Mickey says she finds herself talking to her dead mother, just talking to her and asking her to help her through her grief. Mickey's experience is quite common and quite normal, as are the experiences of Earl and Lakeisha. After a death people also frequently report having very vivid dreams in which the loved person is present and alive. These dreams are often followed by a deep sense of loss when the sleeper wakes up and finds that he has only been dreaming.

Letting Go

Even though you can be intellectually and consciously aware that someone is dead, it takes time and work to let a loved one go. It is important, however, that you do move on eventually, that you gradually "withdraw the emotional capital of the past."[13] That does not mean that you have less regard for the parent who has died or that you must forget him. It means rather that you also need other, living people to love and to share with and that the other members of your family need new relationships, too.

At first it may seem unthinkable that you will ever be happy again. Life seems flat. "Life must go on"; writes the

---

[13] Grollman, Earl A., *Talking about Death: a Dialogue between Parent and Child* (Boston: Beacon Press, 1976) p. 6.

poet Edna St. Vincent Millay, "I forget just why."[14] But with time and grieving life will have more meaning for you. And in some part of yourself you will always carry the memory, the legacy of your parent. "The touch is gone," writes Judith Viorst, "the laugh is gone, the promise and possibilities are gone..., the comforting joy-giving flesh-and-blood presence is gone—[but] it is true nonetheless that by making the dead a part of our inner world, we will in some important ways never lose them."[15]

In Chapter 10 of this book you will be introduced to several people, now adults, who went through the same thing that you are going through when they were teen-agers. Those who lost a parent to cancer all mourned deeply, but they also went on with their lives, completing school, getting jobs, marrying, raising children. All of them still remember their parents and also in some sense are a memorial to their parents in their talents and accomplishments and values. In their lives you will see how a person can keep a loved one with him—and also let him go.

---

[14] Millay, Edna St. Vincent, "Lament," *Collected Lyrics* (New York: Washington Square Press, Inc., 1960), pp. 75–76.
[15] Viorst, *Necessary Losses*, p. 249.

CHAPTER 9

Children in a Single-parent Household

If you are a child in a single-parent household and your parent has been diagnosed as having cancer, you may be feeling particularly vulnerable. You, and other young people like you, have special problems and special concerns. If you lose that one parent, will you have anybody to take care of you, anybody left to you at all? If you have brothers or sisters, will you all be able to stay together as a family if your parent should die? Who will buy food for the family and pay the rent if your sick parent can't earn money any longer? Who will pay for medical care? If your parent goes into the hospital, how will you and your brothers and sisters get to the hospital to visit? If your parent becomes bedridden at home, who will nurse him? Will you be expected to take care of your sick parent all alone?

Compounding all these practical problems is the fact that you, as the child of a single-parent household, have already suffered at least one other major loss in your life. Whether your other parent left the house because of death or divorce or separation or illness or chemical abuse or a jail sentence—or even if you never knew him or her—it is only natural to feel the absence of that parent as a loss. People suffering loss upon loss, as you have, may start wondering what there is in life that they can count on. You may even begin to feel responsible for the bad things, although they are not your fault.

It may also seem at times that nobody else you know has so many crises to face. Why do Jane next door and Jack down the street get to have two healthy parents and a predictable future when your life is such a mess? Why, you wonder, are you always the one singled out for the bad deals? The truth of the matter is that if you explore a little further, dig a little deeper, you will find out how many exceptions there are to that happy two-parent family. All of those variations cannot possibly be touched upon in this chapter, but perhaps you will find in the pages that follow at least one other person whose life you can identify with particularly.

Who Will Take Care of You?

When you are a child, it seems unthinkable that anything could happen to your parents, to the life you have always known. "Before they died," says Charlene, both of whose parents died (one of a heart attack, one from cancer), "I thought my parents were going to live forever." Those of you whose parents have been through a divorce probably also never thought that their marriage could end, that your family could split up. Unfortunately these things do happen, and to the extent that you can see major changes coming—even as a *possibility*—it is to your advantage to plan ahead. Children in single-parent families, more even than others, need to ask the parent they live with what specific plans have been made for their care if anything should happen to that parent. (See Chapter 2.) If the parent you live with has cancer, it is particularly necessary that you find out what arrangements are being made for your future.

Children of divorced parents in most cases still have two parents, even though it may sometimes feel as if you have only one. And both parents are usually able to take on responsibility for their children. If one parent dies, you may be able to live with the other. Remember that your parents did not divorce you; they divorced each other. Chris's mother couldn't get along with her ex-husband and hated his new wife, but Chris and his brother loved their father and thought his new wife would be fun to live with. The reason you are living with one parent and not the other is because *your parents* could not live together, not because your noncustodial parent has bad feelings toward *you*. Your noncustodial parent may be happy to have you, even though he or she may not have been in your life much recently or may have given the parent you live with problems about child support. Divorces get messy and parents often fight about things that are not really the issue. But when a child is in real need and a parent knows that, the picture can change.

But what if it doesn't change? What if you have no parent who can take you? What if your second parent is already dead or not capable of caring for a child? In that case some children have grandparents who volunteer to take care of them; others go to live with aunts or uncles or godparents or even friends. Scott was offered a home by his football coach so that he could finish up his senior year in his school district. Some children, like Charlene who was mentioned earlier, are cared for by a grown brother or sister. But guardianship of a child, even one who is almost grown and will only be in the household for a few years, is a big responsibility. In some cases there is no one the young person knows and no one related to him who is able to take on that kind of commitment. Then the authorities step in and usually place the young person in a foster home, where qualified people can offer him guidance and support until he is old enough legally to live on his own.

None of these alternatives will likely seem the perfect solution, and all will require adjustment and effort and some creative behavior on your part if they are to work for your benefit. You may not need to adjust to a new family at all, of course, if the parent you are living with gets well. But you should still bring up the subject of what will happen to you and discuss it with your parent(s) now to be sure that arrangements are in place. It may seem a difficult topic to get started on, especially with a parent who is ill, but you will feel more secure and be stronger to deal with the day-to-day stresses of your parent's illness if you know that provisions have been made for your future.

Being Your Parent's Caregiver

The question of whom you might live with eventually has to do with the long-term future. But as an older child in a single-parent family, you also need to think about what the immediate future will bring. In a two-parent family when one parent gets cancer, the other parent usually becomes the "caregiver." In a single-parent family an older child may have to take on that role. The caregiver nurses the patient at home, takes the patient to treatments, visits at the hospital, deals with the doctors, and performs various other tasks. Depending on the makeup of your family, you may share this role with brothers or sisters, or you may have to take on your parent's care and do household chores and help out with your brothers and sisters as well. If it sounds like a huge job, that is exactly what it is. It is, in fact, too big a job for a teenager—even an older teenager—to be expected to take on alone.

Finding a Second Support Person

Right now the parent you live with may be the person you go to for support. But what if that parent becomes too weak or too sick to help you, even with issues having to do with his own care? You will need to identify some other adult you feel comfortable with: an aunt or uncle, a neighbor, someone in your church, your other parent, a school counselor, a family friend, a responsible person nearby who can help you with advice and plans and comfort you if the time should come when your parent isn't available to help you. Perhaps you and your parent can even work together to help you identify a suitable person for that role.

Finding a second support person doesn't mean that your parent is giving up his authority, or that you are giving up on him. It is, in fact, a safety measure. And it is just good sense to choose that support person in advance of a crisis. It is also important for you to work out ahead of time specific contingency plans, such as what to do if your parent needs to go to the hospital suddenly, or in some other household emergency. You need, for example, the phone number of a nurse or doctor whom you can contact outside of office hours, because side effects of chemotherapy and radiation therapy can sometimes be frightening and may require immediate attention. You need to know what to do if a younger brother or sister needs medical care immediately. You need a plan in case of fire.

Try to talk about these matters with your parent. Maybe

the support person you choose can be in on the discussions. You don't have to have this other person involved in your life every moment, but someone should be available who can help you when you need help. For your own sake and for the safety of your sick parent and other members of your family, you should plan for these emergency situations ahead of time.

Problems Caused by Loss of Income

As mentioned in Chapter 2, cancer causes financial problems for many families. Single-parent families are often hit harder because there is no second adult to take up the slack when the sick person can't bring income into the house. If the parent you live with is your family's income provider, the prospect of his becoming too sick to work can be particularly frightening. Where will the money come from for doctors and medicine? How will you pay for food?

Teenage children are not usually in a position to earn enough money to support a family. And if you are your parent's caregiver and your parent is too sick to work, chances are he will need you to spend a great deal of time helping out at home. But if no money is coming into the house, how will the family survive?

Be assured that your family *can* survive. What you need to do is to suggest to the parent you live with (who is probably worrying about the same things) that he or she get in touch with a social worker at the hospital or someone at a cancer care agency who can supply information about resources available to get you through. These people can help you figure out where to apply for supplementary income, how to get a hospital bed or crutches or a wheelchair, what bills are covered by insurance and how and when to pay them, how to get food stamps if you need them, and other practical matters. You will get help doing paperwork and filling out forms. The kinds of programs mentioned are designed to help people in times of need, and if your family qualifies for help, it is only sensible to take advantage of them. Some people are reluctant to accept such help, but at least talk to a social worker and get the information you need so you and your parent don't have to worry about what your family is going to eat for the next few months. For people who refuse to accept direct help, arrangements can usually be made to delay paying bills or to pay them off a little at a time until the bread-winner returns to work and money becomes available.

Nursing Care

If your parent's illness gets worse, the question of nursing care will also become more complicated. There is often a period of time—and in some cases quite a long one—when a cancer patient is not sick enough to be in a hospital but too sick to take care of himself, to bathe himself, to fix a meal for himself. Usually if the patient is able to get out of bed enough to use the bathroom, he can stay by himself at least part of the time. When he is alone he may be able to use a system by which an emergency call button or a pre-programmed telephone alerts someone that he needs help. If he needs around-the-clock care but there is no medical reason to admit him to a hospital, some families hire un-skilled help (perhaps a neighbor or an unemployed relative) or a home health aide to be with him during the hours when the family caregiver must work or go to school. It is almost always too expensive to hire a nurse to be with the patient all the time, and most insurance programs don't cover that kind of expense. Nursing homes, too, are usually too expensive. So most families have to find some way to care for the patient at home.

As a teenager, you should not be expected to try to work out these arrangements for your parent by yourself. The best course is to consult with your sick parent about his needs and wishes, and then as a family get in touch with the social worker at the hospital or cancer treatment center where your parent goes for treatment. Cancer care agencies also have experience in dealing with all these problems; if there is such an agency in your area they can help you choose the best and most comfortable arrangement. Or call 1–800–4–CANCER (National Cancer Institute) or 1–800–ACS–2345 (American Cancer Society)[1] for advice on how to start arranging for your parent's care. Many people use these numbers, so be prepared to get a busy signal the first time you call, or to be put on hold. If that first phone call doesn't pay off, don't stop there—make another. Try not to feel overwhelmed by the size of the problems you are facing, and above all don't fall into the trap of thinking that it will be easier to try to nurse your parent on your own. It won't—it will be an impossible task, and neither you nor your parent will benefit.

If you don't feel comfortable about getting in touch with these helping agencies, or if your parent can't or won't get the process started, ask your support person to intervene. You might want to pass along to him or her the information in this chapter.

If your parent is in the last stages of illness, one recom-

---

[1] See p. 12 for NCI numbers in Washington, D.C., Alaska, and Hawaii. When you call a national hotline number, ask for a local or district office number for answers to specific questions about help available in your area.

mendation of the helping agencies might be that you get in touch with Hospice, the organization that helps families care for terminally ill patients at home. If your parent is terminally ill and otherwise qualifies for Hospice care, this might be a good solution for you. (See the section on Hospice in Chapter 8, pp. 123–127.) According to the Hospice rules, someone in the family must be designated and trained as the primary caregiver, and a teenager might qualify as long as he or she is responsible and the patient's safety will not be compromised by the arrangement. Sometimes there can be a primary caregiver not on the premises —an aunt, a cousin, a neighbor, an adult friend who will check in regularly—and the teenage children at home help out with the patient's care. These are not the usual Hospice arrangements, but such a plan might be possible and provide a solution for your family.

The Need for Emotional Backup

As an older child in a single-parent household, your care and company will likely become very important to your ill parent. And the worse his illness gets, the greater that need may be. Although you want to help your parent, the emotional demands on you may seem overwhelming at times. This is another area where your support person can help you. You need someone to replenish your own strength, someone to lean on, to back you up when everything seems too much to handle. You should not, in any case, assume that you have to stay home with your parent all the time or to spend every waking moment with him or her at the hospital. You do not have to take the place of your parent's missing spouse, although it may sometimes seem as if that is what you are being asked to do. It may help to keep in mind that even though your sick parent doesn't have a spouse, he or she does have friends and relatives and neighbors. Your job could be to set up a schedule of visitors for your parent so that the responsibility doesn't always fall on you. Remember also that many patients don't even want company all the time. Talk to your parent to find out how he feels. Ask directly what he or she really wants. Maybe your parent would feel less sad if he knew you were out having fun occasionally, if you didn't try to be available to him all the time.

Sixteen-year-old Michelle remembers the feeling of being trapped by her mother's excessive dependence on her. "I mean, she was sick, but this was when she could still get out of bed and all, and I just had to go out once in a while. I'd say, 'Can I go?' and she'd say yes, but then when I got home I'd get this guilt trip about how she'd been all by herself all night. And one time I was at my friend Kelly's house and I called Mom to ask her one question, and I got, like 'When are you coming home?' and I said, 'After I watch the football game,' and she said, 'When's that?'—and then she started to yell at me and I'd lose my patience because they tell you, 'Go have a good time,' and they feel like, 'Why should you have a good time?'"

In fact, Michelle's mother was very frightened about being sick and was converting that fear into anger at Michelle. She was also using her illness as an excuse for not dealing with problems of dependence left over after the sudden death of her husband in an automobile accident. Michelle talked the matter over with her school counselor, who reassured her that it was not really her responsibility to be her mother's constant companion. Although Michelle's mother refused professional help for her own problem, the school counselor helped Michelle get a neighbor to come and "sit" with her mother several evenings a week. This solution allowed Michelle to leave the house occasionally

without being too burdened by guilt, and it took additional pressure off Michelle by giving her mother another
adult person to talk to.

Caught in the Middle

Children of cancer patients whose parents are divorced
often find that their parents' continuing quarrels with each
other add to the stresses caused by illness. "Mom told me
to buy myself a new sweater for my birthday," says Gerri.
"I knew she wasn't going to get it—she could barely get out
of bed—and she even told me how much to spend and
where to go and to have it gift-wrapped so it would seem
more like a present. I didn't want to, but I was going to do
it for her, but then Dad sent me a present, which was supposed to help out, I guess, only he didn't even know what
size I was any more. When my mother saw it she almost
had a fit. She started crying and all. It was awful, because
she wasn't even really strong enough to cry."

Sarah Ann was frightened about what would happen to
her if her mother died. She wanted to accept an invitation
from her father and his new wife to visit them in New York
because she wanted to have some sense of what her life
would be like if she had to live with her father permanently.
But she was afraid to upset her mother because she knew
how much her mother hated her dad and how jealous she
was of his new family. It finally took the intervention of the
hospital chaplain to convince her mother that Sarah Ann
needed this extra contact with her father during her
mother's illness. Finally, Sarah Ann's mother let her
daughter go.

Susan's worries about money likewise stirred up old
issues left behind after the breakup of her parents' marriage. Susan had been distressed about unpaid bills. "Just

put them in a pile," her mother told her, "and we'll handle them as soon as I'm out of this bed." But Susan didn't see how the bills would ever get paid. One night she got so worried she called her father and asked him to write a check for the gas and electric bill. When her mother found out about the phone call, Susan couldn't believe how furious she was. "She said I had to have more faith in her," Susan reported. "But that wasn't fair, because I do have faith in her. But she wasn't awake last week when they said on TV that they were turning heat off on people for not paying their bills. What are we going to do if she's still sick and they turn the heat off?"

You might think, as Susan did, that if one parent is in trouble the other parent would be the ideal person to ask to help out. But Susan's mother had been battling a long time for independence, and in going to her father for help Susan had hit on a very sensitive nerve. Actually, Susan now admits hoping that her mother's illness might bring her father back permanently, that her parents would see how much they really needed and cared for each other. But it seldom works that way. Serious illness is more likely to make old family problems worse rather than better.

The tension and fear that come with an illness like cancer can make vulnerable people feel more vulnerable. Those feelings, in turn, make them lash out and blame each other. Gretchen's mother, recently divorced, has cancer. Her father, Gretchen's grandfather, had a heart attack. "Mom says that Grandpa's heart attack is my dad's fault," says Gretchen. "She says her cancer is, too. She says they were both started by everything that happened at my house, and she's trying to put a guilt trip on my father. I hate it."

In Kay's family it is her father, who lives in the next town, who has cancer. Both Kay and her mother worry about Kay's dad, who lives alone and drinks heavily despite his illness. "But Dad just won't deal with it; he won't stop drinking," says Kay. "And Mom says she can't help him. Dad says Mom doesn't care or she'd let him move back in with us. Last night he called her and wanted to talk about coming home, and Mom got all upset."

Relationships between brothers and sisters are affected, too. "I can talk to my sister sometimes," says Kay, who feels the need for someone her own age to talk to about her feelings about her father. "My sister changes, though, from liking my father to hating him to liking him. It's just, like—make up your mind—I need to know if I can talk to you or not."

Grandparents also get involved. Lucy's grandmother came to stay with her while Lucy's mother was in the hospital, because Lucy wasn't old enough to stay alone. That, says Lucy, just made things worse. "We couldn't go anywhere except when a neighbor took us to the hospital," she says, "because Grandma wasn't able to drive, so the two of us were cooped up in that hot apartment all summer. And she kept saying things about my dad, and that made me mad, so we spent half the time not talking to each other. And when Mom got home there were *three* of us, and Grandma and I kept fighting over what I could or couldn't do for Mom. She didn't think I could do anything. I was never so glad as when my mother got out of bed and told Grandma it was time for her to go home."

You can see how complicated it gets. Is Lucy's grandmother mad at Lucy's dad, or is she really worried about Lucy's mother? Are your parents thinking about your future, or are they still locked in an old power struggle left over from their divorce? Professionals such as hospital social workers and workers at cancer care agencies have experience dealing with these issues; they have seen families of all kinds deal with the old and new emotions stirred up by a diagnosis of cancer. Just as individuals need help, sometimes families need help also. And frequently it takes an outside person to mediate, to figure out what is really going on.

When Your Sick Parent Does Not Live with You

Children of divorced parents whose sick parent is not the custodial parent may also be in great pain, although with a different set of problems. Conflict between parents may keep you from seeing and being with your sick parent as much as you want to. You may feel guilty and worried about how he is doing on his own. You may feel frustrated about trying to get the truth about your sick parent's condition, responsible somehow for his loneliness and illness, disappointed in the parent you live with for not offering to take him in and nurse him back to health. If your absent parent is remarried or in a new relationship, you may feel jealous of those who will get to spend time with him and care for him in what may be his last days. Or you may still feel so angry about the divorce that you aren't aware of any caring feelings left in you at all.

Your healthy parent's feelings about his or her divorced partner may also have been complicated by the news of the cancer, and adults in emotional conflict can unintentionally take out tensions on their children. If you feel tangled in a web of mixed loyalties, it would be wise to talk to a counselor at school or a clergyperson or some adult who is one step removed from the situation to help you sort out your feelings and understand better what your role is in this complicated relationship. The potential loss of any parent is very painful for a child. You don't have to live with a parent to love him. You don't have to like or admire him in order to be affected by the possibility of his death. Your own needs regarding your absent parent may be very different from those of the parent you live with. You should have a chance to deal with your own feelings so that *you* can feel right about what is going on.

Dealing with Loss in a New Home

The death of a parent is difficult for every child, and every child must grieve for such a loss. As discussed elsewhere in this book (see Chapter 3 especially), grieving and dealing with loss is hard work and takes place over a period of time after the death. Mourning and the pain that accompanies it cannot be avoided and cannot be hurried. Those of you who have new living arrangements after your parent's death have the added stress of doing your grieving at the same time as you are making many other big adjustments. It is hard at first to understand how momentous those changes can be.

Charlene went to live with her older brother, Alan, after her father died. (Her mother had died four years earlier.) "I didn't realize what was going on at first," says Charlene. "I just pushed it aside, like—oh, well, it's going to be a new life, I'm going to get to move in with my brother, things are going to be really cool, I'll get to do things I've never done before because he's really young—we're going to get to do energetic things Mom and Dad didn't want to do because they were too old. So it was more or less excitement rather than mourning. I didn't really deal with it until later when I realized, hey, your parents are gone, you know. This is the result."

It wasn't as easy living with her brother as Charlene had anticipated. It was hard for them both to have him play the parent role rather than the big-brother role. The relationship between a child and her parents is different from that between a child and an older brother or sister.

"My parents were the type of people," explains Charlene, "who will go over the edge for you—you know, Mom and Dad always told me, 'We're your best friends; no one will love you as much as we do; people will love you, but no one will have the feeling of—I'll jump out of the car for you,' and that's how my parents felt. My brother is there for a purpose. You know, he cares about me, but he's not the type of person—I live there, but I have to live as if I'm with someone other than just my parents. You know, you can just expect things from parents and not say thank you and the parents know that you love them. When my brother does things I have to thank him, I have to show that I'm grateful, or else it reflects on me as being not thankful for the things he does, because he doesn't *have* to be there."

Having lost both her parents, Charlene felt insecure about holding on to the new home she had with her brother. She dealt with the death of her parents at first by becoming something of a behavior problem, and her brother, who took his new responsibilities very seriously, responded by cracking down hard on her. "I guess I *was* kind of a discipline problem, you know," says Charlene, "with my parents dying. I just went wild—never really getting into trouble but always being real late, you know, because I always had very early curfews, and I'd always talk off—and Alan would just look at me and he'd get really angry and he'd tell me, 'Okay, you know, what we're going to do is you're not going to stay here; we're going to send you away.' It's like—I have no power over what's going to happen to me. It's not fair that I should be sent away—it's not my fault—I didn't do anything wrong, and I don't want to be sent away from all my friends and everything because

I have a small problem with trying to get used to all this. So here he was threatening me and I couldn't do a thing about it. If he wanted to send me to Juvenile, he could just say the word and I'd be gone. I was really scared, and I was angry that he had the power to just change my life like that."

Three years later, after some painful and difficult times, Charlene is still living with her brother. She realizes now that Alan would never have dreamed of sending her away, that he, too, had to learn to cope with a stressful situation. "We learned how to deal with each other," Charlene says. "We're too much like each other, I guess. He's very stubborn, and I'm very stubborn, only he's in authority over me, and he has the inside track as to, well, 'If you're saying this to me, I don't have to listen to you because you're only sixteen and you don't know what you're talking about.' But I've just kind of learned to grow with it. I've taken on more responsibility with my job and am not home a lot. I had to make the changes—I had to become accustomed to—well, if he yells at me, I just don't say anything, I listen, I look at him, I say, yeah, I understand what you're trying to do, you're not trying to hurt me, you're just trying to help me. I just had to get into the groove of how he lives, because you know, he was making changes, too, becoming a twenty-five-year-old parent. But there's times when I still think—eighteen, here we go, I'm getting out of here."

When Greg's mother died, Greg went to live with his father and stepmother. Greg, like Charlene, reacted to his loss by becoming a behavior problem, and the conflicts that ensued put a strain on his father's new marriage. "I would hear them arguing about me all the time," Greg remembers, "and sometimes I'd wish she'd walk out on him because I figured that was what he did to my mom, but then other times I'd get scared because I'd wonder, what's going to happen to me if this family breaks up, too?"

Fortunately Greg's father insisted that Greg see a psychologist who was able to help him handle his feelings more constructively and to assure him that the violence of his feelings—which had been frightening to Greg—were a perfectly normal reaction to the losses he had experienced. The psychologist continued to support Greg as he went through his grieving process, and he also helped Greg's father see that his own unresolved grief and guilt at Greg's mother's death had been contributing to the strain on his new marriage as much as Greg's problems had. Once these issues were aired and worked through, the tension in the household eased, and Greg was able to find a place for himself within his new family.

Sixteen-year-old Blair was very much relieved after her mother's death when her mother's unmarried sister came to stay with her and her four small brothers. Blair had been worried that the family would be split up, that no one would be willing to take on the responsibility of a ready-made family of five. Blair had always liked her aunt, so she didn't anticipate any problems. What happened, though, was that Blair had become so accustomed during her mother's illness to having her brothers look to her as the "adult" in the family that she interfered whenever her aunt told her brothers what to do. Blair resented it when her brothers asked her aunt for something, and she resented it when her aunt tried to take over her duties and treat her like the teenager she was.

"I was so angry," says Blair, "that I wrote a story about it for English, and I guess it was pretty obvious what it was all about because my English teacher called me in to talk to me. She was the one who made me see that it was time for me to let go and let my aunt do some things for *me* for a change. I had been doing everything for everyone else for so long that I forgot how good it feels *not* to have to go home every night and make dinner for six people."

Chuck's parents had been divorced for several years before his mother got sick, but they had remained friends. So it didn't seem like that much of an adjustment after Chuck's mother died for his father to move in and take over the family. But just when everything seemed to be working out, Chuck's father was arrested on a narcotics charge. Chuck, who had only one year of school left, was permitted to move in with some neighbors so that he could finish school in his own district. But the neighbors couldn't take his ten-year-old sister, so she went to stay with an aunt who lived in another state. Chuck felt really bad about the breakup of his family. At first he said he was angry only for his sister's sake, because he felt that his dad hadn't met his responsibilities to her, but in a support group at school he was finally able to admit that he too felt deserted and full of rage at his father. Seventeen-year-old males as well as ten-year-old girls expect support and care from their parents, and they are not too old to feel betrayed and lonely when a parent lets them down.

Coping Creatively with Foster Care

You may think that the worst that could happen to you if your mom or dad dies is that you would have to live in a foster home. And there is no question that it is hard and very frightening to have to live with strangers. But it will be easier if you don't start out thinking that all foster-home situations are necessarily bad. Many foster parents are very special, caring people who truly feel that they have something extra to offer young people who need a home. If you go into a foster care situation assuming that your foster family wants to be helpful, chances are you will have a better adjustment.

If you are in a foster care situation for a time and find that you are having problems, take a moment to determine objectively how much you are contributing to those problems. Often young people who have been deeply hurt build a wall around themselves to see if someone cares enough to knock that wall down. But then they can't get past the wall themselves without help. If this feels like what is happening to you, talk to your social worker or a counselor at school to see if professional counseling might make things easier for you. It is to *your* benefit to let your foster parents support you emotionally and to try to learn from them what your own parents aren't present to teach you. Your foster parents can't help you unless you let them. If they reach out to you, try not to turn them away. Talk to them. They may be waiting for a sign that you are ready to let them come closer. They may be searching for a way to give you what they can.

If your foster home, however, is not a suitable one—if you are being neglected or abused by your foster parents —you need to find a caring adult to intervene for you. Start with the social service agency that placed you in the home, and don't give up if your complaint is not taken seriously. Unfortunately, adults do not always listen to complaints from teenagers, and you may need to press your case further. If you continue to have a problem, talk to a counselor at school or a clergyperson in your new neighborhood, or even a trusted adult from your old neighborhood. It is easy to give up on yourself when you feel alone in the world and everything seems to be going wrong, but you deserve better than to be abused. (For more information on getting help when you are being abused, see Chapter 5, pp. 70–72 and 75–76.)

Don't Blame Yourself

It is especially important when you are feeling down to keep in mind that what has happened to you has happened through no fault of your own. Your parents' divorce, their death, the inability of a parent to care for you because he or she is an alcoholic or mentally ill or incapable of providing you with a stable home—none of these things means that something is wrong with *you*. You are still entitled to good things in life; you deserve happiness. What is true, however, is that you may have to work a little harder, be a little more stubborn or creative in search of those good things. You may have to adjust your behavior, or get help with your feelings, or find a long-term goal you can work toward. You may need patience to live with an imperfect situation for a time without giving up on life or on yourself. Maybe you can get a job so that you can feel more independent. Maybe you can find in a friend's family the warmth and acceptance you don't find in your own household. Maybe you can find others in similar situations and start or join a support group that can give comfort to you all.

There is almost always a way out of a bad situation. It is not true, as you may sometimes feel, that nothing will ever change, that things can't get better. Reach out to someone who can help you find some new options. Sometimes you need nothing more than reassurance, a change in perspective. Charlene, whose feelings of powerlessness in the care of her brother after her parents' death led her to contemplate suicide, was given that important reassurance about herself by a neighbor.

"Talking to my brother," Charlene says, "was hopeless, like talking to a wall. You talk and you talk and you talk—and to get no response and to have no one listen to you and to feel that you're so naive and young that you have no reason to be listened to—that's a horrible feeling. So I figured if they won't listen to me just talking, maybe if I do something serious enough to hurt myself, maybe they'll stop to think that there's something here, because people don't always look at things from a kid's point of view."

Charlene's next-door neighbor, however, was able to look at things from Charlene's point of view. "I didn't need to hurt myself," says Charlene. "All I needed was someone to tell me I was okay. I needed someone to tell me, you're not a horrible person, you don't smoke, you don't drink, you don't get pregnant, you're a good kid. So what if you don't clean house all that great, so what if you're messy, you're not all that bad a person. I needed someone to say my brother was wrong, that I was right, that he shouldn't be making me feel this way. I needed someone to make me feel good, and in that respect my neighbor really helped me."

When life keeps giving you bad deals and taking away the people you love, it is easy to start feeling that something about you is making the bad things happen. But bad things, as Rabbi Kushner says in his book, do happen to good people. Many good things, however, also happen to good people, and it is important for you to remember (or find someone to reassure you, as Charlene did) that you are a person deserving of good things. Have the courage to reach out to life for happiness—and let yourself find it.

CHAPTER 10

What Lies Ahead: The Stories of Survivors

C an you get through this? Will you ever get back to a normal life? Does the pain ever subside?

The answer to all of those questions is yes. In fact, hard as it is to believe right now, the time may come when the distressing details of this ordeal that you and your family are going through will fade—some may even be hard to remember. That is not to say that you will ever forget a parent who dies, but only that the business of living with illness will inevitably shift from being the focus of your present life to being part of your past. An element of pain will probably always be with you, but in time it will be a different order of pain from what you are feeling today, and it will find its place among the joys and successes and the routine tasks—and even the other griefs—of everyday life. With the perspective of time, you may even find some good things to remember about this period of your growing up.

How can you believe such a thing, when you can't even

imagine it right now? It may help to read the cases below, the recollections and reflections of adults now in their thirties and forties who, like you, had a parent ill with cancer when they were in their teens. They survived, and their experiences are offered to give you faith that you, too, can survive. Remember as you are reading, however, that many changes have been made in the past twenty-five years in both treatment of and attitudes toward cancer.

J. is a woman now in her thirties, a professional photographer who is married and has small children of her own. Her father died of cancer just before her sixteenth birthday. "I was in the ninth or tenth grade—I guess the tenth grade—and my brother was eight," J. recalls. "My father got sick in the fall and died in January, so it wasn't very long.

"Things were very different in the early sixties. Nobody mentioned the word cancer. And nobody was really sure what was wrong with him at first. Then I remember he did have exploratory surgery—I guess at the time the doctors saw what was in there, but I don't think anyone ever said the word cancer. I don't think my father knew, or at least he didn't admit he knew. It was really strange—we were trying to protect him, I guess, because there was so little treatment back then. I don't know if the doctor told my mother he had cancer and she never said it to me, but we never told my father, and I think we kept him in the dark. Maybe he knew the last couple of weeks, but he never said it, he never admitted it.

"At the time, I thought pretending like we did, acting as though he was going to get better, was the only thing to do. In later years, when I looked back on it, I agreed that we didn't handle it right—I don't know, it's hard to say—and I wish that we really did have a chance to talk about things openly and honestly, that we had given my father a chance to at least know what he was fighting against. Maybe we could have talked about more deep, spiritual kinds of things, communicated at a different level. I don't know how well I would have been able to at that age, but I think if we could have handled it maybe it would have been more fair to my father."

J. is easily moved to tears; there is a lot of emotion in her voice when she talks about her father, with whom she had an exceptionally close relationship. When he was alive, she says, she always considered him her mentor. "Sometimes," she says, "I feel as if he is still living through me, because we had a lot of the same interests, and I am doing some of the things he wanted to do. He always told me, for example, that when he retired from his business he would like to have his own photography studio, and I, of course, am a photographer now. A lot of his philosophy, too, I think he was able to communicate through me, and his values, his outlook on life, his ways of dealing with people. . . . There are a lot of questions I would like to be able to ask my father now. I'm always curious about how he would react to different things that have happened in the world. . . . There have been times in my adult life when I've felt a little bit sorry for myself, wishing that I had a father, wishing that my children could see their grand-father. . . . I remember thinking when I was just coming out of college and looking for work that if my father were there I would have a little more leverage in the world. I felt like I had to do so many things on my own. . . .

"It *was* such a great loss, of a person whom I loved and was close to, and I think that was what upset me the most even then. I don't think I worried that much about how we would get along, financially or otherwise, although there was actually no money to speak of when he died. But what I really wanted was him in my life. I remember we cried continuously for several days after he died; we probably cried every day for several months, I guess. But I was also so wrapped up in school, and I was at the age where I was starting to have crushes on boys, so there was a lot for me to be distracted by, so I did those things, too. . . .

"It was incredibly, almost unbearably painful at the time, you know, while he was sick and soon after he died, and I can't remember whether it was a matter of weeks or a matter of months—it was definitely less than a year—but eventually that stopped. The pain does get less intense. And after he died, we liked talking about him, even though it made us cry a lot. We would show old movies and look at pictures and talk about things. Even now I'll see old pictures and old movies and I'll cry, but not to the same extent, of course.

"Sometimes I've felt like my relationship with my son is very similar to my relationship with my father—sort of a mentor kind of thing. He's very interested in my teaching him things, like when I'm working in the darkroom. . . . It's interesting. We were a family of four when my father was alive, and when he was gone, being just three of us was very, very sad. And now that I'm married and have two children and am a family of four again, there's a sense of feeling complete again. Even though I'm in a different role than I was when I was in the last family, in a way there's a lot of similarities. . . . On one level, it's almost as if I'm back in a family again, and the family's complete again, and it's almost like nothing's amiss any more. . . ."

L. is also a woman in her late thirties, married and pregnant with her first child. Her mother, who developed cancer when L. was eighteen, was treated successfully for the disease and is still alive. But L. says that her mother's illness began a pattern of denial in L.'s family that still continues. One of the things L. learned from the experience is that she does not want that pattern repeated in her other relationships.

L.'s mother found out that she had cancer when L. had just gone off to college. L.'s younger brother was still at home. To keep her children from knowing that she had cancer, L.'s mother got up every morning at four o'clock so that she could go for treatment and return before her son woke up. It was a neighbor who unwittingly broke the news to L. one weekend when she was home from school.

"I was in shock," remembers L. "It was the first time I ever swore at my mother. I remember slamming into the kitchen and yelling at her, 'Okay, what the hell is going on here?'"

L. tries to evaluate the experience, which affected her so much at the time that she quit school and stayed home for the year, "although it was the dumbest thing I ever did," she says. "I foolishly thought that if I were closer to the situation, I would understand better what was going on, but by then the treatments were over and my mother didn't have any side effects and the whole thing was treated as if it had never happened." L. says that her parents' inability to share with her made her feel shut out, and she responded in later life, much to her regret, by shutting her mother out of her own interior life, although she remains in frequent touch with both of her parents. L. also responded to her parents' implied message that she couldn't cope by becoming a "super-coper." She ultimately returned to college and went into Hospice work, after which she worked for a cancer care agency.

Although L. is not sure how much her choice of work was connected with her mother's illness, she assumes that it must have been connected in some way. "But I had been fascinated for a long time with the subject of how the dying were treated, because it's such an inevitability, and it has always amazed me that people don't think about it until they have to. At some point you have to deal with it. . . . And I know that as a result of my work, I'm much less afraid of hospitals. I've watched people die. I've watched people dealing with people who are dying. I've got a lot more education than most people have on the subject."

"The coping is fine," L. continues about her self-styled role as "super-coper." "But I do find my time to break down, to go a little crazy at times, because that's what gets you through, and I know, because we've had a lot of other serious illness in our family. I'll take a walk by myself and cry and scream and yell and so forth—the kinds of things I hope my mother does but I don't know if she does or not. I resolved I'd never let my parents do that same number on me—hiding things from me—although they keep trying to protect me from things. Even now, my mother's sick again and they tried not to tell me because I'm pregnant. But I keep fighting them on it. My brother, on the other hand, was never allowed to go through any of the hard times, starting with the first time when everyone denied the cancer, and life is a whole lot harder for him than it has been for me. He's been into drugs and has had problems staying in school, staying in jobs, problems with relation-ships. . . .

"My mom's sick again now," continues L., "although it's probably not related to the original cancer, and if I had a crystal ball I'd say that in five years life won't be as nice for me, that something will happen to one or both of my parents, but I'll survive it. I'm much more prepared now, a lot stronger, because I've had a lot of dry runs. And I also had an extraordinary friend who taught me something.

When something critical happened in my life, he'd take me to dinner or I'd go to his office, and he'd sit me down and say, okay, how are you feeling? How is this affecting you? Where are you going to take this? And when he died a few years ago I think the hardest part was knowing that I'd have to do that for myself. But it's important to do that, to spend some time, some selfish time, assessing where you are and who you have become as a result of a rough situation. Because if I had a message for parents, it would be that—that the opposite of protecting your kids from having to deal with pain and hurt and scary things is giving them something positive as a result, is letting them grow through something tough. But unfortunately I don't think a lot of people see it in that light. . . . "

S., a professional man who is married and has several children, was fifteen years old when his father got sick. The youngest in a very large family, S. had been very close to his father. "Dad was a real outgoing person," S. remembers, "whom everybody liked, and he was kind as the day was long, very good with us kids. He was a boxer as a kid and was a real strong man—not big, but just real strong. I really looked up to him." S.'s father's illness first showed up in loss of coordination, loss of memory, and dizzy spells, and S. clearly recalls his dad's frustration and his own pain at seeing the changes in his once-strong father. He remembers vividly that after he got his driver's license he was expected after school each day to drive his father around to jobs; his father had a plumbing business and didn't want to stop working even after he could no longer get around on his own. "He would get really frustrated and angry about not being able to drive," S. recalls, "and he would get mad at Mom and me. I can remember at least one incident being in the car when he just lost it and started kicking and screaming. He was such a good, good man, but he had never been sick in his life before this. I remember I felt a little scared. I remember him grabbing the steering wheel. I remember hitting the brakes and pulling over to the side of the road as fast as I could. Even at that age I was my full height and about 235 pounds and in much better shape than I am now, so I was big enough to deal with it. But it's hard—how physical can you get with your father?

"I did most of my mourning," S. says, "when Dad was sick. I was the helper in the family—even as the youngest I was the one who stayed at the hospital. I probably got that softer side of me from Dad, but I also have another side, the tough-it-out part I get from my mother. At the very end we had to put Dad in the hospital, but we stayed round the clock with him—he was in and out of consciousness. I was with him the whole night before he died—that was when I was sixteen years old. Those were long nights. . . ."

S. says that his religion helped a lot during those long nights. He had gone to a Catholic high school and had "a very comfortable relationship with God and could pray very easily. I felt confident and good about prayer, and it helped me a lot with acceptance, that I would get through it."

He also remembers that he was able to talk about his feelings with two of his brothers-in-law. "I'm not sure some of my other brothers and sisters had that kind of outlet, that they could talk about it," he says, "and it makes me wonder now if that's the reason for some of the problems they're having. I also think I probably felt some anger sometimes at my brothers and sisters because it was implied that because I was the last one at home I had to do everything—I had to take on certain responsibilities, keeping Mom company, taking her places. . . . When my father died, I'm the one who went with my mother and made all the decisions about the funeral arrangements. When I look back at it I think, why was it me? Why weren't some of them doing it? I'm sure I took on a role of support during the sickness—you know, helping Dad, helping Mom, being with Dad—and I was kind of the companion, not the one who took care of the bedsores and all, but the companion. . . .

"But I also worked and went to school and played football during that time," S. says. "And when Dad died it was my second week in college. I was also busy at work—I would work fifty to sixty hours a week in addition to school—so I had to put it aside real quickly. But I think, as I said, that I had done a lot of mourning by then. I can remember the funeral, and I can remember being with my one brother-in-law who could let me relax and let me cry and let me laugh. I also think what happened—and what does happen in some cases—is that another father figure comes along. In my case it happened to be my boss at the job I had at the time—in a limited way, but he was there, and he became the person who was guiding me in the early stages of the business world—get your work done, get your school done, he would say, and he always would check with me about how school was going. If you're working for someone fifty-sixty hours a week, that person can become a large part of your life, and he did. . . ."

S.'s father's illness was hard to diagnose; it is now thought to have been a combination of cancer and hardening of the arteries. S. remembers feeling a sense of helplessness because he didn't know if proper medical decisions were being made about his father's condition, but he didn't think it was a teenager's place to ask. "I've always wondered how well the doctor looked into it, whether we

were with the right doctor," he says. "As a teen, you don't
have any input into things, but even then I wondered. The
doctor was a GP, and I wondered if he should be doing all
of it—this was in the early stages—but I never said
anything."

S. recalls a time later when his wife ruptured her spleen
in a fall and was rushed to the hospital for emergency
surgery. "I wouldn't let them operate," he says, "not until
we'd got another opinion, and I made sure it was the best
doctor. And do you know, they *didn't* operate—they
decided in the end that they didn't have to? And I think my
doing that was part of that thing with Dad. Do we have the
best doctors? Do we have a guy who cares what's going on?
I guess I've always wondered, was everything done that
could have been done? If everything had been dealt with
soon enough, would Dad have done better?"

S. says that although he no longer actively mourns his
father, he still feels the loss. "I still miss Dad," he says.
"But I miss him more than anything now for my kids
because I would like them to have known him. He would
have been a neat Grandpa. And it's probably been brought
back to me more since my father-in-law just died. You
never stop missing him totally. . . ."

R. was in college when her mother had her first surgery for
breast cancer. "We knew something was wrong probably
about a year before that," R. says, "but she denied and
denied and denied. I think I handled the whole thing as
well as I did because I saw my father handling it the way he
did. I think if a parent—even if it's upsetting—can handle
the physical changes well, then it's easier.

"They told my father six months at first, but she lived for
thirteen years. My parents were both the kind who

said—well, that may be what you say, but that's not the way we're going to deal with it. They were both fighters —my mother especially. I think my father probably got his strength from her attitude, and the rest of us did, too. I was living at home and was included in lots of things. She didn't drive, so I had to take her to the doctor, to fittings for her prosthesis [artificial substitute for a body part]. I was with her four or five years later when she was having trouble walking. She wouldn't go to the doctor but we put up a fuss, and I was there when he said, well, it's cancer again, and—I find it hard now to believe that I went in and just said okay, and we were able to talk about it on the way home. . . .

"I was angry at her, too—I mean, the only reason she went to the doctor was that I sat there and cried—I mean, I had a tantrum, I literally had a tantrum. I said, I can't believe you're doing this to yourself and to us, and it's unfair of you, and if you're scared it doesn't matter because if something bad's going to happen it's going to happen, but if it's going to happen then we have to try to change it. I was twenty-three or so by then, remember—I don't know if I could have done that earlier, as a teenager.

"There were a lot of adjustments. I had to make changes at school. I was supposed to go away to work on a project for a month, and I had to make that change without even knowing that she was as sick as she was, but now I'm glad I did, because I just felt very uncomfortable about being away from home. . . .

"We always kept a sense of humor—that's our family's way of handling stress. . . . When my mother went into the hospital I handed her a couple of magazines with a card I'd made that said, 'While you rest, keep abreast,' and we had a bulletin board in the room that said, 'Recovery or Bust.' Even at the funeral home, when we had to choose a casket, we got the one we wanted and then my father asked them if the casket had a warranty on it, and they started looking for it until he said, 'I was joking...' But in a real tense moment—I mean, you have to be that kind of person, but that was my father's way of not being overwhelmed. And it helped the rest of us, too, because you could laugh at a situation that otherwise would have made you very uncomfortable. But some people have trouble listening to me tell about that and think it's very disrespectful....

"That's the other thing," R. says, "people will say, Oh, can you believe it, her mother's scarcely cold in the grave and she's going to the movies?—well, I think you *should* go to movies. In fact, I like to give people that for a gift when someone dies—I like to give them a gift certificate for two to see a movie, just to get themselves out, to get themselves in the world again. I don't find it disrespectful. I think that what anyone who dies would want is for you to go ahead and live your life.

"If there's a certain mourning period, I think that's great if it works for you, but it didn't work for me. I think you can start moving back into society tomorrow, or even yesterday. I think that's what helped my family, because it was a slow death—that we had so much time to accept dying. I mean, she was home right to the end and when you see someone so sick and lying in bed like that, not conscious—it was so painful to look at—I mean, *you have grieved*, you have done it, you have been through it, you've done your share, and you need to get on with whatever it is that you have to do. My way a lot of times was just to lie down in bed at night and cry for ten minutes. Or I'd think of something and it would make me sad....

"After she died I took my children to the cemetery," R. remembers. "I felt like I wanted to go to the cemetery a lot, which I didn't think I'd ever want—I thought cremation was the way to go—but it was so nice to be able to go and think and just walk through there, and I'd take my kids and I'd give them jars of bubbles. . .and to this day neither of them minds going. We don't go very often anymore. I think my mother knows what a wonderful family I have—I want that so badly. . . ."

"There are two scary things I remember," says R. "One, when my mother came up from surgery. I remember being scared, not because of the breast or anything, because I couldn't see that, but because she looked so *sick*. And she looked, maybe, what I thought would be dead—and I think that was terribly frightening for me, but our rabbi was there at the time and he was wonderful. I remember he said, that's what people look like when they've been through major surgery, and that helped. But I think that was the scariest part of the whole thing. . . .

"And then a few years ago my sister was diagnosed with cancer of the thyroid, and that really upset me. I mean, everyone said, oh, it's curable, it's almost ninety-nine percent curable, but I only heard on one level what they were saying. But she was fine, and that was a good experience, too, because then you learn and you're able to pass on to your children that cancer doesn't have to be death. I know with my mother part of it was that she was so scared—I don't know that she would have died if she'd gone to the doctor right away. . . .

"This weekend we had a birthday party for my father and we put together a slide show," says R., "and there were all these pictures of my mother in her prime, looking beautiful—where I always had pictures in my mind of her not that healthy—I mean, I remembered the years right before she died. But she was looking beautiful, and my sister's children, who only remember her when she was sick, kept saying, Look at Grandma, look how nice she's dressed, look how pretty her hair looks—they were so impressed because they remember her very sick in a wheelchair, without any hair. And it impressed me, too, because now when I think of my mother, I see this slide—this one slide—and she looked *gorgeous*. It's good to go back and have an image in your mind like that—not seeing her in the coffin or when she's very sick."

R. says everyone thought it was so terrible for the family that her mother had died such a slow death. "But I've said all along that there are some good things, too. Actually, I think the worst kind of death for a family is a quick death. It's a terrible situation to go through, watching a person die, but you're ready when it comes, you've done what you need to do, and you can accept it better. And part of the ease in accepting it is that you can talk about it, and you can make peace.

"I mean, I didn't know *when* my mother was going to die, but I remember she was in the hospital the summer before she did die. She wasn't able to breathe, and they called the doctor and he said, Don't worry about it, which may have been his way of saying, Let it end—but my father wouldn't go for that at all, so they called my husband, and he ran over there and got life support and called an ambulance and took her to the hospital, and she was good for a couple of days after that. And while she was there in the hospital I decided I was just going to write a letter and say all the things I needed to say, and I did that and gave it to her. My sister had done the same thing, although neither of us knew what the other one was going to do. Then in another week my mother started losing ground—I guess it was probably affecting the brain, because she started being not real clear—and if I had waited any longer it would have been too late. . . .

"And *then*," adds R., "I went home and wrote a letter to

my father, because I didn't want anything to happen without my being able to do that. That kind of thing was really important—my mother's death was over such a long period of time, and there were many things I did—some by chance—that made it easier. I'm glad I got to do them. I'm glad I got to say goodbye."

You have just heard four stories of four persons, all dealing with the same problem you face now—the cancer of a parent. But different as those four persons are, it is important also to notice what they have in common, because their voices echo some of what has been said in earlier chapters of this book. All of the four remember how essential it was for them to be able to express emotion. They all had someone else they could cry with or be comforted and strengthened by. They all valued times of communication and regretted lack of communication. The three whose parents died have not forgotten their parents but find that the intense earlier pain of loss has rounded off now into a softer, more comforting kind of remembering. And each of the four has a sense that the experience influenced his later life in ways that were positive and strengthening as well as negative.

"But the most important thing," says R. firmly, "is that you feel what you feel. Because kids, like everyone else, deserve the freedom to have the whole range of emotions without any of the guilt. And I think that's probably the hardest thing, because there's always someone out there saying something about your attitude or the way you're doing things. But it's you who have to deal with it, and no two people deal with it in the same way. You do what you need to do to get through. And you make it. There were times when if you had told me that, I wouldn't have believed it. But it's been ten—almost eleven years now. And you get there. You truly do."

CHAPTER ◇ 11

Conclusion

T he assumption throughout this book has been that
you, the child of a cancer patient, will be able to deal
with the stresses of your parent's illness if (1) you
know the truth about your parent's condition and its
potential consequences for you and your family; (2) you
seek appropriate help when the task of coping gets too
difficult; and (3) you explore and express your feelings
about your parent's illness in an open and honest way. You
have been offered examples—present and past—of the
problems other teenage children of cancer patients have
had to deal with and ways in which they grappled with
those problems. But perhaps you feel even more doubtful
now than before about your ability to handle what the days
ahead may bring. Just because those other teenagers could
handle their problems, does that mean that you will, too?
The truth is that you won't know exactly what you have to
face and how you will face it until you see how your
parent's illness progresses. The way you cope will depend
on such things as your own personality, your experience,
the setup and style of your family, your place within your
family, the support you get from others, and the other

things that are going on in your life at any particular moment. If you are afraid, perhaps the best thing to remember is that, as Rabbi Earl Grollman says, "courage is not the absence of fear, but the affirmation of life *despite* fear."[1] You may want to share that thought with other members of your family.

There may even in the end be good things that grow out of this painful experience. You may resist hearing that right now. You may even think at this moment that you are never going to let yourself love someone again since the prospect of losing a person you love can hurt so much. But love can also bring great happiness: Probably you know that, too. And pain is an unavoidable part of everyone's life.

Robert Veninga interviewed physicians, psychologists, nurses, and chaplains who had dealt with people in crises, and they all observed that people are changed by such crises, often coming through them with new purpose and new direction.[2] As one teenage child of a cancer patient says: "I don't like the reasons, but having had my father sick made me a lot more mature, I think, a lot more sympathetic to other people's problems, a lot more aware, a lot more understanding." Sixteen-year-old Maureen also says that she has learned to appreciate people more since her mother got sick: "It used to be, 'I don't want to go to Grandma's house,' but it's not like that any more. Now it's, 'Let's go to Grandma's house!'" Alison says that her family has become better friends all around. "Usually," she says, "you are at odds with your mom, but she needs companionship and because there's a person missing we all need to be close, and out of that need you form a better

---

[1] Grollman, *Concerning Death*, pp. 136–137.

[2] Veninga, *Gift of Hope* p. 5.

relationship, and it's good for all of us. I mean, Mom understands me like a friend, and my friends can't understand me."

The way back to happiness, to healing may be long and painful. Few people who face losing something of value can go directly from the sadness of loss to happiness again. "For most there are many detours, dead ends, and just plain awful days."[3] But it is important, as you have seen, to allow yourself to have those awful days when they come. Face your emotions as they come, the message is, and draw strength from the fact that grieving is also healing. Because, as Lesley Hazleton says in her book *The Right to Feel Bad*, "to experience the full range of emotions, to struggle with the downs as well as to enjoy the ups" is what it is to be fully alive.[4]

Not all of you will know all the heart-wrenching experiences described in this book. For some the path will be easier, your parent's illness treatable, the practical advice on coping with death and funerals and new relationships premature. But even for those who must live through the lingering death of a loved parent, the message is that you can and will survive. You will hurt and you will grieve, but you will also heal. You will pass through this pain and come out stronger on the other side. It won't be easy for you, but you can and will get through these difficult days. And there will be time in your life for happiness once again.

---

[3] Veninga, *Gift of Hope*, p. 69.

[4] Quoted in Gordon, Sol, *When Living Hurts* (New York: Union of American Hebrew Congregations, 1985), p. 30.

PROPERTY OF
SOUTH KNOX SCHOOL CORP.

Bibliography

Atchison, Catherine. "The Forgotten Victims: Children of Terminal Cancer Patients." Northampton, Mass.: Smith College for Social Work, 1984, Thesis.

Adams-Greenly, Margaret, M.S., and Sr. Rosemary T. Moynihan, M.S. "Helping the Children of Fatally Ill Parents." *American Journal of Orthopsychiatry*, 53 (2), April 1983, pp. 219–229.

Bernstein, Joanne E. *Loss and How to Cope with It*. New York: The Seabury Press, 1977.

Bradley, Buff. *Endings: A Book about Death*. Reading, Mass.: Addison-Wesley, 1979.

Brueggemann, Walter. *Praying the Psalms*. Winona, Minn.: Saint Mary's Press, Christian Brothers Publications, 1973.

Bruning, Nancy. *Coping with Chemotherapy*. Garden City, N.Y.: The Dial Press, Doubleday & Company, Inc., 1985.

Furman, Erna. *A Child's Parent Dies: Studies in Childhood Bereavement*. New Haven & London: Yale University Press, 1974.

Gardner, Richard A., M.D. *The Boys and Girls Book about Divorce*. Science House, Inc., 1970.

———. *The Boys and Girls Book about One-parent Families*. New York: G.P. Putnam's Sons, 1978.

Gordon, Sol. *When Living Hurts*. New York: Union of American Hebrew Congregations, 1985.

Grollman, Earl A. *Concerning Death: A Practical Guide for the Living*. Boston: Beacon Press, 1974.

—————. *Talking about Death: A Dialogue between Parent and Child*. Boston: Beacon Press, 1976.

Grunwald, Lisa. *Summer*. New York: Alfred A. Knopf, 1985.

Gula, Richard M., S.S. *What Are They Saying about Euthanasia?* Mahwah, N.J.: Paulist Press, 1986.

Harding, Rachel, and Dyson, Mary. *From the Private Letters of Illustrious People: A Book of Condolences*. New York: Continuum Publishing Company, 1981.

Hazleton, Lesley. *The Right to Feel Bad: Coming to Terms with Normal Depression*. Garden City, N.Y.: The Dial Press, Doubleday & Company, Inc., 1984.

Humphry, Derek, and Wickett, Ann. *The Right to Die*. New York: Harper & Row, 1986.

Holleb, Arthur I., M.D., ed. *The American Cancer Society Cancer Book*. Garden City, N.Y.: Doubleday & Company, Inc., 1986.

Klein, Allen. "Humor and Death: You've Got to Be Kidding." *The American Journal of Hospice Care*, July/Aug. 1986, pp. 42–45.

Klein, Stanley. *The Final Mystery*. Garden City, N.Y.: Doubleday & Company, Inc., 1974.

Kopp, Ruth Lewshenia, M.D., with Stephen Sorenson. *Encounter with Terminal Illness*. Grand Rapids, Mich.: Zondervan Publishing House, 1980.

Krementz, Jill. *How It Feels When a Parent Dies*. New York: Alfred A. Knopf, 1981.

Kubler-Ross, Elisabeth. *On Death and Dying*. New York: Macmillan Publishing Co., Inc., 1969.

Kushner, Harold S. *When Bad Things Happen to Good People*. New York: Schocken Books, 1981.

Kutscher, Austin H. *But Not to Lose: A Book of Comfort for Those Bereaved*. New York: Frederick Fell, Inc., 1969.

LeShan, Eda. *Learning to Say Goodbye*. New York: Avon, 1976.

————. *What's Going to Happen to Me? When Parents Separate or Divorce*. New York: Four Winds Press, 1978.

————. *When a Parent Is Very Sick*. Boston and New York: The Atlantic Monthly Press, 1986.

Levine, Stephen. *Who Dies: An Investigation of Conscious Living and Conscious Dying*. Garden City, N.Y.: Anchor Press/Doubleday, 1982.

Link, Mark, S.J. *These Stones Will Shout*. Niles, Ill.: Argus Communications, 1975.

Linzer, Norman, ed. *Understanding Bereavement and Grief*. New York: Yeshiva University Press, Ktav Publishing Houses, 1977.

Lund, Doris. *Eric*. New York: J.B. Lippincott Company, 1974.

McCoy, Kathleen. *Coping with Teenage Depression*. New York & Scarborough, Ontario: New American Library, 1982.

Millay, Edna St. Vincent. *Collected Lyrics*. New York: Washington Square Press, Inc., 1960.

Moody, Raymond A., Jr., M.D. *Laugh after Laugh*. Jacksonville, Fla.: Headwaters Press, 1978.

Morra, Marion, and Potts, Eve. *Choices: Realistic Alternatives in Cancer Treatment*. New York: Avon Books, 1980.

Index

PROPERTY OF
SOUTH KNOX SCHOOL CORP.